Horses
of
Hollywood

Horses
of
Hollywood

Roberta Smoodin

UNIVERSITY PRESS OF KENTUCKY

Copyright © 2025 by The University Press of Kentucky

Scholarly publisher for the Commonwealth,
serving Bellarmine University, Berea College, Centre
College of Kentucky, Eastern Kentucky University,
The Filson Historical Society, Georgetown College,
Kentucky Historical Society, Kentucky State University,
Morehead State University, Murray State University,
Northern Kentucky University, Spalding University,
Transylvania University, University of Kentucky,
University of Louisville, University of Pikeville,
and Western Kentucky University.
All rights reserved.

Editorial and Sales Offices: The University Press of Kentucky
663 South Limestone Street, Lexington, Kentucky 40508-4008
www.kentuckypress.com

Cataloging-in-Publication data available from the Library of Congress

ISBN 978-1-9859-0173-5 (hardcover)
ISBN 978-1-9859-0172-8 (paperback)
ISBN 978-1-9859-0174-2 (pdf)
ISBN 978-1-9859-0171-1 (epub)

This book is printed on acid-free paper meeting
the requirements of the American National Standard
for Permanence in Paper for Printed Library Materials.

Manufactured in the United States of America.

Member of the Association
of University Presses

For Tim

Contents

Preface
They're in the Starting Gate

Do animals experience emotions as we humans do? Certainly, dogs feel empathy, more so than any other animal species, even more than our genetic relatives, chimpanzees. They are aware of our feelings and are more tuned in to our emotions and visual cues, according to scientific studies. Our belief that human consciousness represents the pinnacle of sentience is both egotistical and demonstrates our own lack of empathy, as we look down on the consciousness of dogs, horses, and cats, our primary domesticated animal partners, as being lesser, if we believe it exists at all. But how sentient are we, really? Most people are listening challenged and so self-involved that we misunderstand even our closest human relationships or make little attempt to understand them, or even ourselves. Our much-vaunted consciousness exists, for a lot of us, as a fog of me-ness from which we attempt no escape.

People who work with animals for a living are frequently not much better, treating the animals they work with as the tools of a job and objectifying those animals as a means to an end. I once had a horse trainer tell me, "Horses are no smarter than chickens." I know better and know that animals communicate with us, but we are not open to this communication, just as we are not open to much of human communication. Our consciousness is overrated due to an inherent narcissism in the human race. Without a self-image, dogs, horses, and even cats are purer beings who seek to be understood by us, trying to make their needs and wants known to us. How stupid they must think we are!

After a career as a writer and professor of English, I discovered horses and changed my life completely. I owned and operated my own Thoroughbred horse farm in New Mexico, Texas, and eventually Kentucky, the Thoroughbred center of the universe, doing all aspects of horse care on my own, as I quickly realized I couldn't count on any hired help to do the job that I wanted done. The help didn't view my beloved horses as individuals in need of special care and instead paid little or no attention to the horses' moods and health, forgetting which mare needed daily medication, for example, to keep her pregnancy safe or to check the water of mares in the barn. So I gave up on hired help and did all of the work myself, from mucking stalls every morning to de-worming, vaccinating, medicating, feeding, watering, and applying first aid. I got my mares and my clients' mares pregnant, kept them pregnant, and then pulled their foals out of them in the middle of the night. The job's hours were insane—the cliché 24/7 literally applies. But I loved them, and I saw each as unique individuals and was able to detect the slightest alteration in their behavior that might indicate impending illness or some type of unhappiness with their living situation. I cared for as many as thirty-some mares on my own during my years on the farm.

Here is what I learned: just as different humans have varying levels of emotional engagement with others and varying degrees of sensitivity, have more or less intelligence, and have more or less ability to feel and communicate their feelings, so too do horses. Some have little personality and desire to engage with humans (perhaps they are the most intelligent!), while others have huge emotional capabilities and desire to engage and, clearly, just like dogs, love. They also get angry at real or imagined slights, become happy about the offer of caresses or treats, and come running when you call them, just because they are thrilled to see you and to receive and return the love you have to offer. If you pay attention, you can learn much about horses by knowing their eyes. Their eyes will tell you if they're feeling unwell, if they're unhappy, if they're ready to play. There is indeed sentience in a horse's eyes, and there are real emotions in their personality repertoire.

Like most horse people, I love movies about horses, but I require more from them than most viewers, probably because of my years spent critically analyzing literature, teaching, and writing novels. I don't want to see horses as no more than cowboy-mobiles, unfeeling brutes only good for transportation. I want to see horses who display emotional intelligence, who truly act, much as human actors can replicate necessary emotion. Horses that clearly have feelings about the situations they find themselves in and can communicate that emotion. Is this a Hollywood horse trainer's trick? Or do horse trainers search for those special horses, some of whom I have experienced, who are more willing to display emotion and intelligence? Through the writing of this book, I've come to appreciate the talents of a gifted few horse trainers who clearly share my feelings about horse emotion and do their damnedest to display it on film. But just as with humans, there are better actors and worse actors; a good trainer can improve the performance of a worse horse, but the Olivier or De Niro of horses can elevate a trainer from masterful to brilliant.

This, then, is my thematic requirement for good horse films and bad horse films: horse sentience. Though I also bring my working knowledge of horses to these films and am frequently disappointed by ignorance (if not idiocy) about horses and writers/directors who should know better but don't, I'm willing to swallow a certain amount of misinformation if the main horse is a great actor, just as I'll watch Adam Driver or Brad Pitt in any film they make. The combination of physical appeal, which comes naturally to just about any horse, and ability to communicate both self-knowledge and other knowledge, trumps all else for me, and it is my desire, through this book, to display for readers both truths about horses and the reality of profound horse emotion that I have experienced.

So close your eyes and imagine that we are about to wander through the Movie Horse Hall of Fame, in which horses who can act are celebrated. A stuffed version of the famous Trigger, Roy Rogers's horse, stands in the lobby, and various wings feature paeans to such horses as Rex, Joey, Secretariat, Seabiscuit, and many others. Ridley Scott has his very own wing. And the great horse failures, in which movies pathetically portrayed horses as mere conveyances, have their own wing, the Hall of Shame. I hope none of your favorites are stabled there!

1

Muybridge and the Wonder Ponies

As testament to the forever intertwined history of the movies and horses, the very first motion picture was, arguably, made in 1878 of Kentucky-bred mare Sallie Gardner galloping. Eccentric millionaire, railroad magnate, and ex-governor of California Leland Stanford (and founder of prestigious Stanford University) commissioned a mad, brilliant photographer, Eadweard Muybridge, to investigate the mystery of equine movement. Legend has it that Stanford had a $25,000 bet with another restless millionaire that, when a horse is running, all four feet were off the ground at the same time, creating what Stanford called "unsupported transit." More likely, however, is that Stanford's passion for breeding better American Standardbred trotting horses on his eight-thousand-acre ranch (that later became Stanford University) would be benefited by a more profound understanding of the engineering of the horse's gait.

Eadweard Muybridge (1830–1904) was born Edward James Muggeridge but changed his name to reflect what he considered to be the original Anglo-Saxon version of his family's name. Muybridge, born in England, immigrated to the United States in 1855, eventually opening a bookstore in San Francisco and leading an orderly, normal, well-groomed life. In 1860, after Muybridge had decided to return to England for a visit that same year, the stagecoach in which he was a passenger had a deadly accident, falling off a rocky cliff near the Texas border, killing two and injuring all the other passengers. Muybridge hit his head on a rock and remained unconscious for nine days; after awakening, he had no sense of taste or smell, remembered nothing of his accident, and was forever altered. Due to the traumatic injury to his orbitofrontal cortex, the once pleasant Muybridge developed a terrible and instantaneous anger, a lack of care for his personal hygiene, great bouts of melancholy, and moments of comatose placidity. Those who had known him before found him irretrievably altered. Injury to the orbitofrontal cortex is still considered a causative factor in obsessive-compulsive disorder, and a physician urged Muybridge to take up photography (as a ruse to get him out of his sickbed and into nature, which the doctor felt might be curative). The now wild-haired and wild-bearded Muybridge—whose hair had turned completely white in the first three days after his accident, resembling Walt Whitman in his dishevelment—began an endless quest to capture the natural landscape, notably of Yosemite, with his camera. He became a famous photographer, thanks to the type of traumatic brain injury suffered by professional football players, thought to be the cause of suicides and murders among them. It would cause something similar in the irretrievably injured Muybridge and perhaps account for his genius.

At the age of forty-three, the now-addled Muybridge married a twenty-one-year-old shop girl named Flora Shalcross Stone and had a son with her. Even before their son was born, however, Flora had grown discontented with her older obsessive/compulsive husband, who only wanted to take photographs, and began attending the theater and other social events, which led to her meeting drama critic Harry Larkyns, with whom she began an affair. Photographs depicting her and her son were discovered by Muybridge among love letters Flora had written to Larkyns, and on the back of one, she had inscribed "little Harry," driving Muybridge into one of his black furies. In 1874, Muybridge bought a gun and went to the site of a poker game Larkyns was known to be attending and knocked on the door; when Larkyns answered the door, Muybridge said, "I've got a message from my wife," and shot Larkyns point-blank in the chest. Put on trial for murder, with insanity as his defense, testified to by many medical experts and friends, Muybridge was acquitted by a jury of older white men, who cited not Muybridge's craziness but appropriate human nature as the cause of their finding: they believed that, in similar circumstances, they too might have committed a justified homicide. So much for the rule of law. Muybridge, fearful for his own life because of the murder of such a popular society dandy, exiled himself to Central America for a year, taking photographs all the while. When he returned, Leland Stanford contacted him to commission him to photograph his horses.

First, Muybridge attempted to discover the mystery of the horse's gait by photographing a trotting horse, Occident, owned by Stanford, but the very slow shutter speeds of the heavy cameras of the day captured only a blurry dream vision of a horse in motion. Muybridge's psychotic brilliance and imagination seized hold of the problem with the tenacity of a terrier, and he invented a mechanical shutter that only took one-thousandth of a second to close. He then installed twenty-four of these cameras with rapid shutters on Stanford's racetrack at his enormous ranch in Northern California, twenty-seven inches apart and timed to shoot at successive intervals of one-twenty-fifth of a second apart. The cameras were connected by thread tripwires to poles across the track so that when the horse broke the thread, the cameras' shutters opened and closed.

This time, the race mare named Sallie Gardner, ridden by jockey Gilbert Domm, was the subject, and the timed photographs created what today we consider a flip-book; when one flips through the photos, the figures in the images appear to be in motion, as in a movie. Indeed, Muybridge discovered what Stanford suspected: that all four feet of a horse were off the ground at the same time, gathered up under the horse, which happily surprised Stanford. Muybridge then invented the zoopraxiscope, a device like a movie projector that

Eadweard Muybridge (1830–1904) serial photo of jumping horse, 1887. (Photofest.)

showed the images on glass plates, one after the other, depicting the horse's motion more effectively than the primitive flip-book. Thus, the mare Sallie Gardner became the world's first equine movie star.

Of course, Muybridge became obsessed with his inventions and took serial photos of raccoons, cats, chimps, dogs, humans dancing, a woman crossing a stream by stepping on a series of stones, and many others, and he became a world-renowned figure, traveling through the United States and Europe to demonstrate and lecture on moving pictures. He showed his invention to Thomas Edison (1847–1931), out of whose head the proverbial light bulb popped at the thought of better moving pictures. In France, the Lumière brothers and Georges Méliès were similarly inspired.

A contemporary of Muybridge, Dr. Étienne-Jules Marey (1830–1904) was a doctor of both medicine and physiology and the inventor of the sphygmograph, a precursor to the device that is used to this day to measure blood pressure, among many other inventions. What really fascinated Marey, however, was human and animal motion, especially that which the human eye was unable to see clearly. Before Leland Stanford commissioned Eadweard Muybridge to attempt to photograph horses in motion, Leland Stanford had read Marey's book *La Machine Animal*, published in 1873, and it piqued Stanford's interest in that which was unseen in horse movement.

Surprisingly, Muybridge actually visited Marey in Paris in 1881, during one of his European lecture tours. Marey was aware of Muybridge's amazing "moving pictures" of horses that demonstrated exactly what interested him, movement invisible to the human eye—in this case, the horse with all four feet off the ground, gathered up under. While Muybridge was a brilliant photographer, Marey's interest was more purely scientific, and he felt there was much to be learned about animal and human movement and physiology through such ventures.

The very next year, 1882, Marey invented a strange camera that he called the chronophotograph; it resembled a small Gatling gun and, when pointed at a subject and "fired," exposed forty-eight plates in seventy-two seconds. However, he rapidly moved on to a camera that resembled other early recorders of moving pictures. Of course, among his first subjects were horses, though he is most famous for his photographs of a cat falling and landing on all four feet (1894). The difference between Marey's studies and Muybridge's was that while Muybridge focused on actual moving pictures, Marey's work was ghostly photographs, multiply exposed, so that the flow of motion of the horse (or any other animal) appeared in a single photo. The resulting image had a haunting quality, like looking at a single horse and a herd of horses at the same time.

Though it is impossible to know with any certainty, I would wager that Auguste Lumière (1862–1954) and Louis Jean Lumière (1864–1948) may have attended one of Muybridge's European lectures, touting his new moving pictures, or at least were aware of him and his discovery, as their family business in France was in photographic equipment. They were also almost certainly aware of the futuristic work of Marey, with his multiple-exposure photos. Because of their profound knowledge of existing photographic processes and equipment, the notion of moving pictures must have fascinated them. They created their own Cinematographe Motion Picture System, which would record, develop, and project motion pictures and, on March 20, 1895, debuted their first ten short films at the meeting of the French Industrial Society in Paris. It is known that another great French early film pioneer, George Méliès (1861–1938), attended this meeting, and after viewing the Lumières' work, abandoned his career as a magician to make moving pictures.

These first ten moving pictures were each less than a minute long and depicted such regular human activity as gardening, blacksmithing, feeding a baby, and goings-on at the main square in the city of Lyon (filled with carriages and wagons pulled by horses). But the one that stands out from the others is called *La Voltige*, an archaic French word for trick horse riding or circus-type acrobatics. In its forty-three seconds, *La Voltige* features an unbelievably patient black horse, held by a groom, wearing a strange girth-type device with handholds on it, for mounting the horse bareback. Two men attempt to mount the horse, and the first fails miserably. Then the second man, outfitted all in white, makes his first feckless attempt, falls off (the groom's hilarity ensues), and then tries again and again, each time failing in a different manner, falling off both sides of the horse and ultimately ending up sitting with both legs hanging off one side of the horse. It becomes clear that the man in white is some kind of acrobat and that this whole routine has been choreographed. Once again, the horse was notably the perfect subject for the infancy of moving pictures.

The Lumière brothers patented their moving picture system on February 13, 1895. American inventor Thomas Edison invented, with the help of photographer William Kennedy Dickson, the kinetograph, a device to record moving pictures, and the kinetoscope, a peephole viewer for short films at penny arcades. He believed this small-scale viewing represented the future of motion pictures, but the Lumière brothers understood that movies needed to be big. Thus, on horseback, through the horse's gift of elegant movement, the movies were born.

Hollywood's romance with the old West was born at the same time as silent movies (*In Old California*, 1910, is considered the first silent movie made in Hollywood), and movie cowboys were the earliest heroes of the silver screen. Viewers who loved westerns wanted to know more about the horses, which were frequently far more expressive and interesting than the stone-faced cowboy heroes such as William S. Hart (1864–1946). Hart's horse was the first movie horse to get a screen credit under his own name—Fritz (1907–1938). Fritz, the first so-called Wonder Horse, appeared in numerous films, such as 1915's *Pinto Ben*. Fritz the Wonder Horse performed all his own stunts, and though he was originally owned by producer Thomas Ince, Hart acquired him for himself during contract negotiations—he dearly loved that pinto pony. Fritz got fan mail, which he always answered. Fritz made twelve movies with Hart between 1914 and 1924, until Hart decided he loved the little red-and-white pinto gelding too much to continue risking his life in dangerous stunts, which had injured both Hart and Fritz numerous times. Hart even wrote a book, *Told under a White Oak Tree*, narrated by Fritz, recounting their adventures together. For a dangerous jumping stunt in the 1920 film *Sand*, Hart had an exact double of Fritz created, the first mechanical prop of this kind. Hart had himself and the "stunt double" suspended from a ceiling with piano wire; when the wire was cut, both fell from what appeared to be a steep cliff. This stunt looked so realistic that Hart had to appear before censors, who were certain that a living horse must have died in the shooting of this scene.

Tom Mix's Tony, who some believe was the first nicknamed Wonder Horse, was owned and trained by the cowboy star and was arguably smarter than most denizens of Hollywood at that time, only having to be shown a trick once to master it. He was also a drop-dead handsome Tennessee Walking Horse, a sorrel gelding with four socks and a wide blaze, and he starred with Mix (1880–1940) in over three dozen films. Bought for a bargain $600 by Mix in 1917, from a Sioux chief according to one account or from another actor/stuntman in other lore, Tony (1910–1942) died exactly two years, to the day, after the death of Mix in a car accident, the victim of supposed colic and euthanasia. Tony was known for his intelligence and was quite the actor, given the gift of sentience in his films, demonstrating that he understood language, vocalized in reply, and responded to commands in an instant. He also appeared in a circus and Wild West show with Mix when the cowboy got tired of Hollywood and took a hiatus. Tony, of course, went with him.

Gallant Bess (1947) and The Adventures of Gallant Bess (1948)

When a horse gets top billing, above even the human stars, that horse must be pretty special. In *Gallant Bess* (1947), the equine is the star: Bess the Wonder Horse is clearly the focus of the film directed by Lew Landers, and the gorgeous sorrel Quarter Horse with a blaze face and four socks reportedly knew over two hundred tricks and worked off verbal commands from her owner/trainer, Joe Atkinson. In a bit of very contemporary gender confusion, Bess was played by a gelding named Silvernip, though the horse insisted, through counting out letters with his hoof, that he preferred to be called OT. Bess/OT first appeared in a 1946 MGM short entitled *The Horse with the Human Mind* that featured Atkinson showing off all of OT's tricks (all manners of vocalizing, nodding yes or no to answer questions, hat stealing, bowing, playing dead or dying, balancing on slender boards and even rearing on them, and many more) and included a visit with other MGM animal stars, Leo the Lion and Lassie. This was followed by Bess/OT's first starring role in 1947's *Gallant Bess*, playing a dual role of both the original Bess and the subsequent Bess, whom her young owner, Tex Barton, finds on a Pacific Island during his service in World War II, after the heartbreak of the original Bess dying of pneumonia. Andrew Marton directed the Wonder Horse in this film and featured all of her/his tricks. In one terrific scene, Bess protects Tex from forest wildlife, including a squirrel, a skunk, a raccoon, and, finally, a mountain lion with evil intent. In this scene, Bess/OT demonstrates a commonly seen bit of equine behavior, the Flehman response, in which a horse lifts its head and bares its teeth, in a gesture of what seems like distaste. The skunk inspires this in Bess/OT, and, indeed, in reality the Flehman response is a horse's reaction to an interesting or unusual scent. The horse has an extra organ for its sense of smell, a vomeronasal organ behind its palate, and the Flehman response is no more than the horse sucking the unusual scent into its miles of nasal passages and multiple nasal organs and then into its brain, in an attempt to comprehend the smell. Use a shampoo with a new smell and feed your horses, and the horses will engage the Flehman response to attempt to understand why you smell different.

Gallant Bess was supposedly based on a true story about horse love found in the jungles of the Philippines by a young member of the Army Corps of Engineers. Tex Barton (played by Marshall Thompson, who would go on to star in the television series Daktari, on TV from 1966 to 1969) leaves his beloved mare Bess, in foal, behind when he goes to war, though no amount of expert acting by the gelding OT could communicate this pregnancy realistically. After six months away from Bess, Bess/OT had no expanding belly due to pregnancy. When the original Bess becomes ill, Tex gets leave and returns home only to see Bess die and bury her. He sinks into an endless depression, and the previously mild-mannered young man seeks out conflict through which to express his anger. Then he finds the injured mare, the new Bess (though still played by OT, dyed a darker color and with only a star on his forehead), who becomes the good luck charm for his outfit and even saves his life when he is shot by a Japanese soldier. The new Bess uses the trick Tex taught her to lie down next to him so that he may pull himself onto her back and be taken back to his unit's sick bay. Tex's despair when he is ordered home knows no bounds, but loyal Bess swims out to the ship and climbs on to go home with Tex. And to have a beautiful sorrel foal, though I cringed when the foal tried to nurse from Bess/OT. Luckily, this scene was brief, and it isn't known if the foal lived through this attempt.

In the subsequent star vehicle for Bess/OT, *The Adventures of Gallant Bess* (1948), Bess/OT is a wild horse that two ranch hands are attempting to capture for their boss, the evil Millerick. Once they do, Ted Daniels, one of the hands, falls in love with her, even saying, "It was love at first sight" and "Bess was in love with me." Ted quits his job rather than give Bess up to Millerick, and he teaches her all of her two hundred tricks, only to have his leg broken when Millerick plots against him in a rodeo. While Ted recuperates, Millerick gets Bess and uses her as the star of his rodeo and Wild West show, taking credit for all her well-learned tricks, dressing her up like a cheap Las Vegas showgirl, and getting her to perform by using a studded whip. Of course, Ted gets Bess/OT back and on top of that gets his doctor's beautiful daughter as wife, truly the man who had it all. Ted is played by a young Cameron Mitchell, who rides like a champ and who, at only thirty years old, before his face turned into something that belonged on Mount Rushmore, is nearly unrecognizable here—and unremarkable, as Bess/OT is the true star.

Bess/OT got hundreds of fan letters a month, which were answered with a glossy black-and-white portrait stamped with a hoof mark. It's unclear what happened to Bess/OT's burgeoning movie career, though it is known that Atkinson performed live shows with OT demonstrating his intelligence and amazing ability to do just about everything, including counting, spelling, and anything else Atkinson wanted him to do.

Clearly, horses were an inspiration to early filmmakers and early film audiences. Once Muybridge discovered and filmed their elegance of motion and graceful beauty, the movies fell hopelessly in love with horses. Is there anything more glorious than a man or woman on horseback who can really ride? In films and television, too, cow-boys and their horses were popular; consider Roy Rogers and Trigger (now stuffed and inhabiting the Roy Rogers Museum in Oklahoma), the Lone Ranger and Silver, and, of course, the talking horse, Mr. Ed; however, I don't like the limitations and stupidity of television's treatment of horses. The movies underscored the unbreakable bond between man and horse, a unique devotion and romance.

2

Rex, the Devil Horse

A coarsely handsome horse with a masculine head and keen eyes stands at the edge of a rocky cliff, looking over his domain. Rex is thinking. Rex—the King of the Wild Horses, the Wonder Horse, the Devil Horse—was the first animal actor to get top billing in his films, made from 1923 to 1938. He also made half-hour serials, in which he received top billing over Rin Tin Tin. Although Rex was perfect for silent films because of his expressive acting that needed no sound, his career was not impacted by the arrival of sound, like those of so many other silent-film actors who fell by the wayside because of unpleasant voices or an inability to deliver lines convincingly. Rex's acting didn't depend on anything but his own charisma and his apparent ability to understand what his part was and to fulfill his character's emotional and intellectual longings. Rex was also the ultimate badass, as mean a horse as ever lived. He may have killed as many as three men, though studio publicists and their lore are not to be trusted. His attempts at murder were witnessed by many, on many a film set, to the point that when Rex wasn't in a scene, he had to be locked in his trailer to suspend his reign of terror and uncertainty amid the mortal, human actors. Rex is said to have earned over $100,000 for his various owners over the course of his career, a very large amount of money indeed in the 1920s and 1930s.

Rex was born on May 1, 1915, in Rochelle, Texas, at Richard Sellman's Mountain Vista Ranch. Until Sellman's death in 1925, the best Morgan horses in the world were bred there. A Morgan horse is a breed that came about via breeding together Arabian horses, Welsh Cob horses, and Friesian horses to create an intelligent, small (usually around fourteen hands), big-boned riding horse much fancied in the early parts of the twentieth century, though rare now. Rex, who stood sixteen hands tall, was an anomaly, a monster of a Morgan, though his bone structure and strong, noble head bore the mark of one, as did his dark coloration. His registered Morgan name was Casey Jones (#6255 in the Morgan Registry), by Headlight Morgan and out of the mare Nannie L., a truly blue-blooded pedigree.

There are several stories told about how Rex got into movies. One is that at two, Rex was sold to a Colorado rancher, and his career in assassination allegedly began when he killed a wrangler attempting to break him. Because of this, the rancher gave Rex to the Colorado State Reformatory for juvenile delinquents, and the first juvenile delinquent who attempted to ride him supposedly came back dead, dragging on the ground with one foot still in its stirrup. At first sentenced to death for his transgressions, Rex was instead kept in a dark stall for two years, his only contact with humans occurring when the youths came to taunt him and spit on him. Years later, his trainers discovered that if they spit in Rex's direction, he would rear up and paw the air in anger, which turned out to be one of his best and most frightening tricks.

Trainers Charles "Chick" Morrison and Jack "Swede" Lindell were hired by movie producer Hal Roach to find a horse to star in a movie about wild horses. Morrison had heard of a fearsome horse in Colorado (where he too owned a horse ranch), and he bravely went, with Lindell, to meet the horse stabled at the reformatory in 1923. The horse, originally acquired by the reformatory for breeding purposes, was virtually wild, but Morrison and Lindell saw something in him, a spark of extraordinary intelligence and personality; so they bought him for $400 and brought him to Hollywood. It should be noted that Morrison was killed by his favorite horse, Young Steamboat, who fell over backward on Morrison while he was training him in 1924, so his instinct for trainable horses veered toward the impossible; indeed, he admired Young Steamboat for his wildness, just as he admired Rex, and paid with his life.

At this time, Lindell became Rex's sole trainer for the rest of the horse's career. Only three men ever rode Rex in the movies, one being the greatest horse stuntman ever, Yakima Canutt, whose face bore a scar for his whole life from where Rex savaged him. Another was cowboy star Hoot Gibson, who rode Rex once, which was more than enough. The third, probably a stuntman, is unknown, though Rex is rumored to have killed a stuntman in 1931. Actor Harry Carey Jr., who knew Canutt well, has told what he claims to be a true story of the interaction between Canutt and Rex. Supposedly, after meeting the killer horse, Canutt had the stunt department tie his wrists and ankles around Rex's neck and barrel and then instructed them to let the horse loose, to prove to the horse that he had to respect Canutt and that Canutt could not be thrown and murdered by the terrifying Rex.

An alternative origin story for Rex's film career is that Morrison heard of a "devil horse" who lived at a riding school in Golden, Colorado, and at Hal Roach's behest, went to see him. Considered unrideable, Rex was sequestered in this tale, too, to keep him from killing people. So the provenance of Rex, after he was sold to the Colorado rancher in 1917, remains a mystery. Though Rex is rumored to have died in the 1940s, his death was also recorded to have happened when he was twenty-four years old, putting the date in 1939. Upon his retirement after his 1938 film *King of the Sierras*, which was incomplete at the time and completed later with a different cast and crew, Rex fathered a few foals, some of whom were used for movies, though none could approach Rex's acting ability and intelligence. Fred Jackman directed all six of the original Hal Roach–produced Rex films; because of the horse's untamable nature, Jackman shot lots of footage of Rex just being Rex—carousing with mares, running through rugged country, getting into fights with other horses—and then used whatever fit into each particular movie. Rex would, supposedly, respond to the sight of the whip in his trainer's hand by charging toward the trainer aggressively, although once he got so mad at Morrison for an unknown equine-perceived slight that the whip didn't stop him, and he ran both the trainer and cameraman over. The Rex epic saga also included recurring roles for other animals: Lady, the white mare, who played his lifelong love; Marquis/Marky, the pinto, who played The Killer, Rex's sworn enemy with whom Rex had spectacular fights; and two small burros, for some comic relief, along with various other creatures. Rex also had a double, a calm gelding named Brownie, who stood in occasionally when riding was necessary or when scenes with another animal, such as Rin Tin Tin, nearby, necessitated interaction, as Rex didn't like dogs and was likely to murder Rinny on the spot.

Think of the scene in *Goodfellas* (1990) in which Robert De Niro sits at a bar alone and is visibly thinking about options he has, the violence he might inflict on the world. The first time I saw that scene, it gave me goose bumps, because it isn't De Niro thinking evil thoughts; it is clearly the character, Jimmy, thinking. The real De Niro has disappeared into the character completely. This was Rex's métier. His ability to think and feel as Rex the King of the Wild Horses cannot be disputed. Think too of *Sunset Boulevard* (1950), in which the silent-screen actress Norma Desmond (Gloria Swanson) says, "We didn't need dialogue. We had faces." In many ways, Rex was the ultimate silent-film actor, who emoted more believably and subtly than the greatest human silent-film actors. Rex's love for Lady, his hatred of The Killer, his hatred of bad guys, and his oneness with the wild become motifs in all his films. His intelligent nobility can never be questioned. He did need anger management therapy, however.

Rex's first film, in 1924, was *The King of the Wild Horses* (he made fifteen films and three serials). As in many of Rex's films, a cowboy witnesses The Black, this time fighting a white horse mercilessly, and vows to catch and break him. Billy (Léon Bary), a cowboy for the wealthy Fielding family, becomes obsessed with The Black, with his untamed mane and forelock and his stature as the leader of a herd of wild horses, and does eventually capture him and break him. The wild look of Rex compounds the romance of his character but must have been necessitated by groomers' inability to make him look civilized and remain alive. Pulling Rex's mane and trimming his forelock would've taken massive sedation, which was not yet safely available. The putative plot involves John Fielding's worthless son, who schemes with the ranch's manager to steal his own father's cattle and horses to sell them, which Billy must reveal because of his love for Mary Fielding, the rancher's pure and good daughter. But that all becomes secondary to Rex's flaring nostrils, endless watchfulness, flicking ears, and eventual devotion to Billy, who teaches him that humans can be kind, as, when trapped in a forest fire, Billy rescues him. Rex demonstrates understanding of this rescue and is grateful. The best stunt is Rex jumping over a bottomless gorge, across a precipice from one jutting rocky mountain to another, a shot Jackman was lucky enough to catch while filming Rex endlessly. Rex was fearless about water and, in another great scene, rescues Billy from certain drowning in a rushing river, jumping in without hesitance to save his pet human.

In scenes with Billy and Mary, Rex remains remarkably calm and kind, but if one pays close attention, what is actually transpiring is that Billy has, in his pocket, endless treats that he slips to Rex regularly so that the scene may be shot without injury to the actors. In another common trope in the Rex films, Billy tries to allow Rex to return to his herd and to the wild, in celebration of his untamable nature, but Rex refuses and returns to his human. At least until the pocket treats run out. This same year, Hal Roach Studios made a short entitled *Animal Celebrities*, starring Rex, with Rin Tin Tin appearing in a secondary role. Rex was indeed the King of the Wild Horses and the King of Hollywood.

Rex's next film, *Black Cyclone* (1925), cemented his stardom and popularity, as it grossed $4 million, an unheard-of amount at that time. The cowboy enamored of the wild black horse this time is Jim Guinn ("Big Boy") Williams (who later in his career became one of Errol Flynn's sidekicks, along with Alan Hale), who rescues Rex from quicksand, garnering Rex's eternal gratitude. Jim has been forced to camp out of town after the local bad guy, Joe, tries to kill him, to eliminate him as a romantic rival for the beautiful and pure Jane. In a twinned plot, Rex loves Lady, the white mare and Jane's horse, but when first forced to fight The Killer for her, Rex loses, and The Killer spirits Lady off to join his herd of mares. Human emotions are constantly ascribed to Rex—gratitude, sadness, love, loyalty—and he expresses them all brilliantly.

The film begins by tugging at our heartstrings, as Baby Rex's mother is killed by a rattlesnake, and he is left alone and abandoned, a situation of great peril to the spirit of any horse, as horses depend on their herds for survival, but especially for a sensitive young fellow like Rex. He learns quickly how to fend for himself, even attempting to imitate a bear by scrounging a hive for wild honey, for which he is immediately sorry and is forced to jump into a river to rid himself of angry bees: another human trait for Rex, learning from watching others.

Rex's heroism in this film knows no bounds. When Lady escapes from the clutches of The Killer and attempts to run to Rex, she exhausts herself in her fearful running and is set on by a pack of wolves who see her as an easy meal. Rex, noble head in the air, staring off into the distance, senses the danger his love is in and goes to rescue her, stomping and rearing and sending the wolves packing. In another scene, sleeping Jim is menaced by a cougar who thinks a buffet has been arranged for him—until Rex awakens to fight and stomp the cougar to death.

Joe, the bad guy, has kidnapped Jane and has evil intent; the possibility of rape is a continuing occurrence in the Rex films among humans, though here it is doubled by The Killer's possession of Lady. As Jim fights Joe for Jane's honor, Rex, breathing smoke, fights The Killer again, and this time is triumphant, just as Jim is. The now adult, experienced Rex can lose to no other horse. Yet despite these ugly relationships, Rex's film career thrived.

Yakima Canutt, about to costar (with secondary billing, of course) with Rex, recounted that Big Boy Williams was nearly killed by Rex during the filming of *Black Cyclone*. The horse knocked Williams down and seemed prepared to stomp him to death with gusto, when horse trainer Morrison stepped between them and began raining whip blows on the horse, forcing him to reconsider his murderous intent. Another incident reported from around the same time was that Rex grabbed a young woman at Universal Studios and tossed her over a fence. Rex's patience was limited, and when he needed a break from acting, he truly needed a break. As Canutt said, it's that one extra take that gets someone killed.

In *The Devil Horse* (1926), the last film Morrison worked on before his death, Rex's origin story is once again investigated, in heartbreaking detail. Part of a wagon train west, young Dave Carson (played by director Fred Jackson's son) has a pet orphan colt who is making the trip with the family. The colt, Baby Rex, has known nothing but kindness and love and is gentle as a cocker spaniel.

The wagon train is attacked by Indians (as they are called in the film), who slay everyone but Dave, who has hidden himself from the ambush. But the Indians rope and take captive the colt, Baby Rex, treating him roughly for the first time in his life. This experience ignites in the horse a profound hatred of Indians that lasts the rest of his life. Nothing delights Rex more than killing Indians. Years later, we meet Dave, now grown and played by Yakima Canutt, and we see, for the first time, Canutt's signature stunt, in which he jumps from his own horse to a set of out-of-control horses who are pulling a wagon, the same stunt that is later repeated, to dazzling effect, in *Stagecoach* (1939). The ever-imaginative Canutt did this stunt with help from an extended step attached to his off-camera side stirrup—invisible to viewers, of course. Even knowing that, this stunt is an amazement. Canutt could do anything with and on a horse.

When Dave is captured by Indians, they decide to sacrifice him to the Devil Horse, who escaped from their herd and turned wild and continues with his Indian-extinction program. They tie Dave to a tree in the valley the Devil Horse inhabits and sneak into the underbrush to watch their bête noire murder Dave. In a later (though previously filmed) scene, Dave calls Rex into the fort to bring ammunition in. Jackson required take after take of this, and Canutt could see that Rex was becoming cantankerous and bored. For the final take, when Canutt summoned Rex, the stallion attacked, having decided the debacle was Canutt's fault. He ran at Canutt and, jaws agape, grabbed him by his jaw and neck, tossing him. Canutt rolled away from Rex's striking hooves numerous times after hitting the dirt, with Morrison unable to stop his killer stallion until Canutt was able to roll over a bank and escape with his life.

Needless to say, Canutt did not relish the thought of doing numerous takes with Rex loose and himself tied to a tree, helpless, even with the hidden rope attached to one of Rex's hind legs that was used in most scenes in which Rex acted without other restraint. So Canutt took the horse to a nearby riding arena for some attitude recalibration, using a bullwhip and a pool cue to keep the maddened stallion away from him and to gain some respect from the horse. After that, Rex and Canutt were best friends, and the scene with Canutt tied to the tree went smoothly, with Rex recognizing his long-lost human, Dave; untying him; and letting Dave mount him and ride away. Another mind-blowing stunt occurs when Dave is forced to jump from a cliff, ninety feet high, into a raging river to escape Indians; Rex jumps in after him to save him from drowning, with Rex's water skills put to the test one more time.

Much as in *Black Cyclone*, there are twinned themes of romantic triangles and the suggestion of possible rape; this time the human side entangles Dave and his love, Marion, and the Indian chief who lusts after her, Prowling Wolf. When Prowling Wolf kidnaps Marion, all hell breaks loose. The paint stallion The Killer is the chief of the Indian herd, and just like Prowling Wolf, he covets the beauteous mate of Rex, the white mare Lady. Clearly these were times when miscegenation, both human and equine, existed unapologetically. Rex fights The Killer as Dave fights Prowling Wolf, and good prevails over evil; no white females are befouled by either human Indians or Indian horses. The fight between Rex and The Killer is spectacular and didn't result in murder in real life because both horses were shod with rubber shoes and had layers of gauze over their teeth. There was no training Rex to fake a fight, and I'd imagine both horses still had injuries as, at this time, no humane association watched over the health of animals used in filming. Throughout, Rex's acting remains superb, his wild face demonstrating consternation, worry, happiness, and anger, as his ears flick and his nostrils flare; sentience clearly lives in those fierce black eyes.

Though a lesser movie for Rex aficionados, because the human plot becomes prominent to the detriment of the film, *No Man's Law* (1927) features a famous sequence in which Rex rescues a young damsel—Toby (Barbara Kent), who is bathing in a pond—from two rapacious bad guys, one of whom is a smirking, growling young Oliver Hardy as Sharkey. The bad guys are in the process of attempting to steal a gold mine from Toby's adopted father when they glimpse Toby bathing seemingly in the nude (a flesh-colored swimsuit was used). Sharkey takes her clothes, ties them into knots, and challenges her to come out. Rex comes to the rescue, chasing Sharkey off a cliff; Sharkey is unharmed though scared half to death. When Sharkey's henchman, Jack, takes his turn at attempted rape, Rex tosses him into the water while Toby escapes. Then Rex, the hero horse, defender of femininity, escorts Toby safely home.

Later, the outlaws attempt to kill the prospector in his own mine but only succeed in breaking his legs, and tension ensues when they take the prospector prisoner from his own home, along with Toby, for whom both have evil intent. Ultimately, when Sharkey attempts to throw the crippled old man off a cliff, Rex rescues him, chasing Sharkey off. The second bad man, Jack, played by James Finlayson, decides against attempting to rape Toby, and with little more than that onetime change of heart, she falls in love with him (a strange turn of events to modern viewers, perhaps). Rex, enraged by Sharkey's murderous, rapacious intent, stomps him to death, displaying the intensity of his anger at Sharkey's attempted misdeeds. The use of rape as a given in so many of Rex's films is disturbing, and in Rex's world, it seems that all pure young women are in constant danger, just as Rex's mate, the white mare Lady, is. Being female and white in Rex-world is not an easy gig. That Rex, the devil horse, becomes the protector of all femininity provides a bizarre irony.

Unlike John Gilbert and many other silent-film actors, Rex made the transition to talkies with ease. Sound allowed him to vocalize and emote even more, and even in his old age, he remained a nimble and athletic actor. Along with his films, Rex made serials, and in 1935, he appeared in a twelve-part one titled *The Adventures of Rex and Rinty*. For Rex aficionados, this show is wonderful and addictive, as both horse and dog act spontaneously (or apparently so), with visual cues coming from trainers off camera allowing the animals to seem entirely self-directed. And both animal stars are serious badasses. Rinty (the famous Rin Tin Tin) is no cuddly pup; he is Rex's equal in his hatred of villains. He attacks bad guys over and over, growling and snarling in rage, and suffers as much traumatic brain injury as any NFL quarterback, as the bad guys repeatedly whack him on the head with various cudgels to get him off.

What is wonderfully bizarre about this serial is that it begins in, and returns to, a fictitious Asian island country named Sujan, a short flight from the Philippines. Clothing outfits in Sujan are a combination of heightened Eastern crossed with space-alien couture, with skyscraper hats. Wisely, citizens of Sujan worship horses, and Rex is the god-horse of the island, with his own royal guardsmen, all on white horses, who care for his esteemed personage 24/7. This is the role Rex was born to play—a god.

The American bad guys visiting Sujan for an unknown reason, as Sujan has no visible industry or tourist attractions, except for

Rex, are shown Rex and immediately conspire to kidnap him and bring him back to the States with them. The ostensible reason for this is that Rex is the only black Arabian stallion in the world ("He's worth a fortune!"). This is absurd on many levels. For one, black Arabians are not unknown and exist plentifully in the real world. Second, Rex is so clearly not an Arabian. His Morgan horse head, masculine and large, in no way resembles the effeminate dish-faced Arab head, nor does his stout body have the prancing elegance of the Arabian breed. Rex would never be mistaken for an Arabian, but consensus in the film is that he is not only an Arabian but also sui generis. As well, strangely, the Americans want Rex for polo, a sport unheard of in exotic Sujan, where the fashion code would seem to eliminate the possibility of athletics. Nevertheless, Rex is kidnapped and brought Stateside. Seeing the Sujanese bowing and genuflecting to Rex, who haughtily enjoys the worship, makes the serial well worth watching.

Rampant Rex escapes from the Americans when he arrives in the United States and runs wild in a forest, where he meets Rinty, a homeless dog who is described as having near human intelligence, which is an understatement. Poor Rinty has gotten a foot caught in a painful trap, and Rex, after surveying the situation, frees Rinty from the trap with hoof and mouth. They become best friends forever, and soon Rinty repays Rex, who gets trapped in an abandoned mine, tangled in ropes left there, a seemingly hopeless situation. But Rinty has already made friends with a blond Dorothy Bruce (Norma Taylor) and her polo-playing boyfriend; the dog goes to her and entreats her to follow him, spinning and barking and looking longingly in the direction of his doomed friend. Together, Dorothy and her boyfriend free Rex as the mine caves in. The humans, enraptured by the godlike Rex, decide to break and train him for polo. The boyfriend, Frank Baxter (Kane Richmond), is the good guy of the piece, willing to do anything to save Rex from the bad guys and return him to his rightful land, after a few successful and exciting chukkas of polo, at which Rex, being a god-horse, is a natural.

The plot ricochets between Rex being rekidnapped by the bad guys, who aren't above murder to get their horse; Rex being sought by Pasha, a Sujanese sent to America to recover him (and who has some kind of mind meld going on with the high priest back home); and Frank recapturing Rex. Endless peril for horse and dog transpires, and it becomes clear that their main enemy is not the bad guys but rope! Damn that rope! Both Rex and Rinty are continually getting tied up, entangled, and nearly hanged by that pesky stuff, with dog rescuing horse, horse rescuing dog, and Frank Baxter rescuing both animals at various points along the way. In a world without rope, this serial's drama could not exist.

After many encounters with rope and bad guys, Rex makes it aboard a boat to Sujan, with the help of Frank, Dorothy, and Rinty, to return to the high priest; however, after the boat has arrived in Sujan, the protagonists discover the bad guys have followed them to regain the priceless Rex. A mutiny among the priests of Sujan occurs, with the object being to replace Rex as the god-horse, and for reasons unknown the returned Rex must go through a trial by fire, as a true god-horse wouldn't perish in a fire. Once again, Frank comes to the rescue (along with rope, fire is the secondary danger throughout the serial). Peace is made in Sujan, and Rex is returned to his lofty position of god-horse with his retinue of guards on white horses (not an Arabian in the bunch). Frank is rewarded by the high priest with the prize of Rex's firstborn foal, yet another Baby Rex and yet another priceless black Arabian who is a chip off the old god-horse block.

The serial is plagued by continuity errors and impossible cliff hangers. For example, Frank seems to get shot by the bad guys while trying to lead Rex onto the boat. For some reason, at this one point, Frank and Pasha are powerless to control Rex, and we think we see Frank hit by a bullet, clasp his chest, and fall off the ramp into the water. But at the start of the next episode, we learn that Frank has only fallen off the ramp, and it is Pasha who has been fatally shot. Not fair, but getting patrons to return to their neighborhood theaters week after week had its price.

Throughout, Rex and Rinty are absolutely the stars of the serial, emoting, vocalizing, and even playing dead when necessary. Rex was twenty years old when making this serial, but he still looks great, with sound only enhancing his acting ability. Although some of his oeuvre may be lost and he may be all but forgotten, Rex may be the greatest movie horse ever. Undoubtedly due to his unpleasant personality, and also to the fragility of movie studios, Rex was traded to many studios and didn't enjoy the comforts of a permanent home until his retirement in Sedona, Arizona, and I'd bet he didn't make many friends along the way. But all girls love bad boys, and horse girls love bad horses. The story of Rex is one for the ages and is unique because the star and best actor are clearly the horse; the humans remain secondary and at Rex's disposal. Even Rin Tin Tin is a subordinate character, though he would become, later, one of the great dog heroes of television.

As a postscript, as a child I lived on the same block as a wonderful man, Frank Barnes, who trained Rinny (what Mr. Barnes called him, not Rinty) for TV. Mr. Barnes seemed to love bringing Rinny out onto his front lawn when children were walking home from elementary school, and he allowed we kids to fall all over Rinny, hugging and kissing him. Rinny was always perfectly well behaved and had the same imperial nature as Rex: he seemed to believe that all this adulation was his due. My early interaction with Rinny on Mr. Barnes's front lawn inspired my lifetime love of animals and worship of them as profoundly emotional and intelligent beings.

3

John Wayne, the Godfather of All Movie Horses

When we watch early westerns from the 1930s, knowing that moving pictures were still in their relative infancy and sound even more so, we come to realize the reason John (Duke) Wayne's stardom was practically insurmountable. He took up the full screen with his height and breadth (in his prime, he was six feet five and weighed 230 pounds), and though his acting may have been wooden early on, he was relaxed in his own skin, at ease, and his voice had enough western twang to make him believable as a cowboy and a tough guy. His style of acting—namely, being himself—accentuated his strength of personality. Plus, he was a natural on a horse, especially for such a big, bulky man. Wayne, born Marion Morrison in 1907 (and died in 1979), was a 1930s version of a superhero. His stunts on horseback were thrilling, and his horse in many of his 1930s films, Duke, superb. But these stunts and this horse were able to thrill us thanks only to an actor/stuntman/assistant director named Enos Edward (Yakima) Canutt (1895–1986), whose early career as a champion rodeo star and chance meeting with Tom Mix made him the godfather of the western stunt. Canutt played Wayne's Native American sidekick or a villainous cad in several of these early westerns, trained all the horses in these films, and invented almost every stunt, risking his life to make them happen. Canutt broke every bone in his body and injured every internal organ he had making these films, but he also inspired many of the most moving horse shots and stunts of filmmakers from the period, primarily John Ford. Wayne even supposedly studied Canutt's western twang and his rolling, masculine walk to develop his lifelong character in movies, and the two were good friends for life. It's unclear how Yakima Canutt came to be himself: the myth of the nickname is told several ways, including in an erroneously captioned newspaper photo. Although he was from Washington State, he wasn't from the Yakima River Valley, and his ancestral roots weren't in the Yakima tribe. He was from Scotch Irish and German Dutch stock, and all he ever wanted to do was rodeo, breaking his first bronco at age eleven, quitting school after elementary education, and becoming a professional bronc buster and bulldogger at sixteen. Before Canutt, errant cowboys in movies got paid three to five dollars a day to ride and fall off horses (if they were lucky, a box lunch was included); Canutt invented the profession of stuntman and embodied it with his fearlessness and his ingenuity.

The child John Wayne, still named Marion Morrison, supposedly rode his family's mare, Jenny, to school every day, making horseback riding second nature to him. Whether this is true or not is immaterial. The big man could really sit a horse. Born in Iowa and raised in Southern California, he played football for the University of Southern California until he lost his scholarship due to a broken collarbone sustained while body surfing. Thanks to his coach, who knew Tom Mix, the strapping young man was hired by Fox Studios to do odd jobs and act as an extra. That broken collarbone altered the universe of American movie history. Weighing a whopping thirteen pounds at birth (his poor mother!), Wayne remained a whopper his whole life and took up space on the silver screen like no one before him or since. But a lot of his popularity was due to his relationship with westerns and horses. His horses remain mythic favorites, with their own legends of lies and half-truths, and deserve awards for carrying his strapping frame around, including an honorary mention for the game little Appaloosa Zip Cochise in *El Dorado* (1966).

Conspiracy theories about the equine Duke, named after his famous rider's childhood nickname, abound. Was there only a single Duke? A double with a nearly invisible brand on his hip? A third with a motley face, or was this one merely the first or second with some facial rain rot or other fungal issue? To me, it makes no difference. Duke got top billing, along with John Wayne, in 1934's *The Star Packer* (as well as in some of his other 1930s films: *The Telegraph Trail; Ride Him, Cowboy; Haunted Gold; Somewhere in Sonora;* and *The Man from Monterey*), so his stardom was already assured. And besides, he was completely adorable. Duke, who appeared to be an Arabian or Arabian/Quarter Horse mix, did not suffer fools well. In fact, he was downright cranky. He frequently pinned his ears when Wayne gave him a nudge with legs, reins, or stirrups to indicate that the enormous man on his back was unwelcome. He swished his tail. He narrowed his eyes in discontent. In *The Man from Monterey* (1933), forced to ride, with Wayne aboard, next to a second-tier character on a donkey, he harassed the donkey mercilessly, whacking him with his head and attempting to bite him to demonstrate his disappointment at having been twinned with such a low-rent version of a noble steed. But in that same movie, when a character asks Duke to "go to Morgan's camp and get him and his boys," off Duke runs without a rider, and the next scene has him showing up for Morgan's waiting men, turning around, and leading them back in the direction whence he came. This horse was an organizer who could carry out missions of life and death on his own. His sentience, not to mention his leadership ability, could not be questioned.

Duke was trained by the aforementioned legendary stuntman Yakima Canutt, who also appears in *The Star Packer* as Wayne's Indian sidekick, complete with terrible wig and pidgin English. Canutt was magical with horses, not a horse whisperer like Buck Brannaman, but an ex-champion bronc rider who understood the mechanics of the horse and of western equipment and was brilliant at creating slight changes in tack and organization of coaches so that horses and humans could do almost anything without being injured or killed.

Stagecoach (1939)

Canutt's (and therefore Wayne's) signature stunt was the runaway stagecoach. Though there is a runaway stagecoach in both *The Star Packer* and *The Man from Monterey*, the ne plus ultra of this trope occurs in *Stagecoach* (1939), the film that made John Wayne a huge star. It was directed by John Ford (1894–1973), the quintessential western director who recognized Wayne's charisma early on. The frenzied galloping of the team of horses pulling the stage is magnificent. The perfectly matched dark bay horses strain at their bondage and run as if their lives depend on it, and their hooves echo like bass drums. How can you not love them? The Andy Devine character shakes their reins and calls out their names, "Baby, Brownie, Bill, Sweetheart," in perfect cooperation of man and horses, and nothing seems amiss here. The horses know their jobs: to strain and run and pound, all six as one.

Then, the Indians, Geronimo's band of fearsome Apaches, attack with arrows and guns, arriving on more pounding hooves. One intrepid lone pinto horse, galloping hell-for-leather with Yakima Canutt aboard (again in Indian garb), pulls right up alongside the lead stagecoach horse, in perfect synchronization. The Indian (Canutt) urging the pinto on then begins the thrilling stunt. He jumps, uncertainly, from pinto to stagecoach horse. Failure would certainly mean death. Canutt bobbles for a moment, seems about to fall into the middle of the team of horses, then regains his balance, and rides the left lead horse. (This stunt was possible thanks to an unseen-by-the-camera special stirrup devised by Canutt that he could use to step toward the horses.) Wagon master Andy Devine is shot and loses the reins, putting the stagecoach at the mercy of this lone Indian, with his band following him. All is chaos and turmoil that only John Wayne can transform. An homage to this famous stunt appears in the 2011 film *Cowboys and Aliens*, when Jake (Daniel Craig) jumps from a galloping horse onto the wing of a low-flying alien spacecraft, the stunt choreographed by contemporary horse trainer without equal Bobby Lovgren, who demonstrates his knowledge and love of film history.

Wayne pulls himself out of the coach window and onto the top of the rampaging stagecoach (with Canutt doubling him, as the star can't be risked in this maneuver), sees what has occurred with Devine and the Indian, and furthers what may be the most famous stunt ever in westerns. He shoots the Indian off the lead horse and then leaps onto the hindmost horse, which is still running ferociously. He stands, leaps again onto the middle horse, and then leaps once more onto the lead horse the Indian had been riding as the Indian falls beneath the marauding horses, surely to be trampled to death. Canutt plays both the Indian doing the deadly fall (though a mannequin rigged to look like the Canutt character was the one actually trampled) and Wayne saving the day. How did no one die making this movie? Only the magic of Yakima Canutt can make this appear so treacherous and thrilling. For this stunt, he designed an extra-wide coupling for the horses; with three feet instead of inches separating them (though, thanks to the camera angle, audiences are none the wiser), Canutt is able to fall between them and emerge from the stunt unscathed. Audiences had never seen anything like this before. Who can help but adore these frenzied, trick horses?

What may be the other most thrilling staging of horses and men working in perfect unison on screen, the chariot race in *Ben-Hur* (1959), was also choreographed by Yakima Canutt, and it is a variation of the runaway stagecoach theme. Ben-Hur's horses are a diminutive white Arabian-looking team (harkening back to the cranky Duke), while Masala's horses are big, black, and butch. The shots of them pulling their chariots at top speed are equally thrilling as those of the stagecoach horses, and the shots of their gorgeous heads, lined up in a slight skew so all may be seen at once, have been stolen by many stunt creators because of its beauty. What equine majesty, controlled by one small mortal human.

Once again, Canutt skews reality by placing invisible small ramps and chutes in the stadium, allowing chariots to wreck without human injury. Ben-Hur (Charlton Heston) must jump a wrecked chariot with his team and nearly falls to his death in doing so (Canutt's son Joe doubled Heston for this stunt and was injured doing it, lucky to escape with his life), while Masala's chariot can't avoid the mayhem and wrecks as well, sending Masala (Stephen Boyd) beneath the trampling hooves of another chariot's team. If you don't find yourself holding your breath throughout this sequence, you're not living. The prerace parade of charioteers must also be loved: eleven chariots, each with teams of four matching horses, parading in perfect lockstep around the full circle of the arena. Canutt designed transparent linkages between the lead horses of each chariot to ensure the perfect formation. For horse lovers, *Ben-Hur* is nearly an overdose of mythic horseness and a cousin of Canutt's work in the Wayne westerns.

Even Wayne himself wasn't immune to the charm and personality of his horses. He insisted that no one else be allowed to ride his favorite horse from his later movies, Dollor (supposedly the equine star of *True Grit* [1969] and *The Shootist* [1976], among many others), a handsome chestnut Quarter Horse, whom the Duke loved. How Dollor came to be spelled that way is one of the great mysteries of film history.

Later, Wayne retired Dollor to a family farm in Texas, where the horse was fed only the best imported alfalfa and had John Wayne's album *America: Why I Love Her* played for him daily, at which he would prick his ears and listen with pride. Some accounts, however, state that there was another white-faced chestnut steed named Dollar who doubled nefariously for Dollor in later movies.

However, I must dispute this mythology: the horse in *True Grit* is a different horse than the one in *The Shootist*, with a wider white blaze on his face and more socks. I intuit a publicist's sense of a

Chisum, 1970. John Wayne aboard one of the many incarnations of Dollor. Directed by Andrew McLaglen. (Warner Bros. Photofest. ©Warner Bros.)

good story here rather than reality. *Chisum* (1970), *Big Jake* (1971), *The Cowboys* (1972), *The Train Robbers* (1973), and *Rooster Cogburn* (1975) feature a similar, though not identical, chromey chestnut horse who was supposedly Dollor; however, if these two were the same, it would seem he was able to change his socks and facial markings at will. Be that as it may, Wayne clearly preferred a big, stout chestnut horse, fancied up with white markings, once he got over his eponymous white horse, Duke.

The Searchers (1956)

Perhaps the best Wayne/John Ford film made was 1956's *The Searchers*, a film about rancor and racism conquered by familial love. With Ford, Wayne becomes a character always based on himself, and this tale of redemption is filled with the dramatic scenery of Monument Valley in Arizona. Ford reuses the same rock formations and mesas over and over throughout the trip, though Wayne's character, Ethan

Edwards, is supposed to be covering vast quantities of ground in his search for his niece, kidnapped by Indians who slaughtered the rest of her and Ethan's family. Wayne rides his usual big, stout chestnut Quarter Horse with three socks. Clearly Wayne believed that he looked best on such a huge fancy mount, as this had to be before the time of Dollor. The intrepid horse never falters or demonstrates ill humor as Duke (the horse) did, and though he is not much more than decorative scenery, he cuts a fine figure with Wayne on his back. The immortal line Wayne utters, "That'll be the day," is a testament to his own stubborn willfulness as Ethan, and we fear what may happen when and if the niece is finally found. Though no intense horse stunts are featured and the horses function as mere cowboy-mobiles, the iconic sight of Wayne on his chestnut horse on this mythic quest defines the drama of *The Searchers*.

Similarly, in *The Shootist* (1976), Wayne's last film, Dollor shines as a decorative object. An elegiac film about both the end of an era and the end of a man, *The Shootist* portrays Wayne as J. B. Books, a famous gunman with terminal cancer. Directed by Don Siegel (1924–1991), famed for making *Dirty Harry* (1971) with Clint Eastwood in that actor's career-defining role, this film features a good performance by Wayne. Clearly Wayne needed a masterful director, like Siegel or Ford, to guide him into giving his best performances, allowing him to bring his character to life. The same wrangler/stuntman worked on both *The Searchers* and *The Shootist*, Henry Wills, who seemed to have filled Canutt's shoes for Wayne, but his work doesn't have the thrilling patina of Canutt's. Still, one can't help but love whichever avatar of Dollor works in each film because of his flashy beauty. As someone who has always been a sucker for a horse with lots of chrome, whether the horse is bay or chestnut, I find just getting to see Wayne on Dollor a cinematic treat.

El Dorado (1966)

The anomaly among Wayne's horses may also be the cutest, the aforementioned Zip Cochise in the 1966 film *El Dorado*, directed by Howard Hawks (1896–1977), who made two other versions of the same film for reasons no one understands, *Rio Bravo* (1959) and *Rio Lobo* (1970). Even considered alongside Robert Mitchum and a young James Caan (with three-inch lifts in his shoes so he doesn't appear to be from munchkinland playing next to Wayne and Mitchum), the small Appaloosa horse Zip Cochise is the best part of the movie. He is uniquely marked, with his hind half being a white-and-black spotted blanket and his front half a flea-bitten gray, the two perfectly bifurcated by Wayne's fancy Spanish-style silver-encrusted saddle and stirrups. Zip Cochise was born in Idaho in 1957 and was a famed cutting horse before his film career; he may have belonged to director Hawks at the time of filming. The little horse could act. He demonstrates deep concern when Wayne is initially shot and falls off and once more when, as a result of that bullet embedded in his spine, Wayne falls off again. Zip Cochise, eyes soft, attends to the supine Wayne by lowering his nose to him, as if to sniff out life or death. In another scene, when Wayne faces the sneering villain and his henchmen, he gets the little horse into reverse to leave the ranch, so he doesn't turn his back on this bunch of Ed Asner's men. No head wrangler or stunt coordinator is listed for this film, but the presence of Joe Canutt among the stuntmen suggests that Yakima Canutt did that job, as he did for Hawks in *Rio Bravo*.

True Grit (1969 and 2010)

It's interesting that the Coen brothers (Joel, born in 1954, and Ethan, born in 1957) chose to remake the classic *True Grit*, though, of course, making a much more noir version of it. The original revivified John Wayne's career, and the line "Bold words for a one-eyed fat man" is unforgettable and is even used in the Coen brothers' version. But the original is a creature of its time, and much of it has been softened, sanitized, and sentimentalized. The Coen brothers' version is truer to the original novel by Charles Portis. In it, Mattie loses her arm because of a rattlesnake bite and loses her horse, the beloved Little Blackie. The horse John Wayne rode in the original, Bo, was his favorite horse of all time, and he rode it in several other movies, including *The Shootist*, if Hollywood mythology is to be believed (though there are conflicting reports, as noted, that this was Dollor). No one else was allowed to ride this horse while Wayne was alive. The original version, directed by journeyman Henry Hathaway and adapted from the Portis novel by Marguerite Roberts, blacklisted in the McCarthy era, has charm on its side, something the Coens almost never worry about, and is much loved by movie purists.

All of the characters in the later version of *True Grit* (2010), led by Jeff Bridges as an even more irascible and unkempt Rooster Cogburn, are much tougher, dirtier, and more realistic, and the stilted period dialogue gives the film a stylized feel in line with what viewers who love the western genre have thoroughly enjoyed thanks to *Deadwood* (2004–2006), the HBO western series beloved for its profane and fanciful dialogue. The Coen brothers' discovery of Hailee Steinfeld was genius. Lore has it that they looked at fifteen thousand girl actors before settling on her, though she had no acting experience. But her somber, serious mien and sense of purpose are perfection, especially when compared to Kim Darby's much girlier Mattie, who tries too hard to be cute. Hailee Steinfeld has no cute in her; she has the energy of a hungry shark on the hunt. As well, Matt Damon is wonderful as the Texas Ranger LeBoeuf, while Glen Campbell, in the original, is simply dreadful. But I am mainly interested in the horses!

Little Blackie must be considered one of the great horses in film, though not in literature. In the book *True Grit*, the horses have no personality whatsoever, and even worse, the heroine, Mattie, is an obnoxious, controlling, small-minded brat. The story is told in the first person, from her point of view, and she quickly wears the reader out with her pronouncements and opinions. One does not wish to live in her head. The story begs for a distanced narrator, like Nick Carraway in *The Great Gatsby*, who observes the heroine and has about him perhaps an ounce of humor or adult realization. But no. Thank goodness, in both films made from this book, the filmmakers' point-of-view rules, and fortunately for the viewer of the Coen brothers remake, Coen-world is a vastly more realistic place than Portis-world.

The Coens' take allows us to adore Little Blackie and his connection with Mattie, invisible in the book. Heroic and sympathetic, Little Blackie carries our heroine through the action and gives up his life for her in the later version of the film. Tears are guaranteed. Certainly this is a variation on the girls-and-horses theme, but it is also so much more. In the Coen brothers' version, the heroic horse, carrying both Cogburn and Mattie, dies trying to get his mistress to a doctor before she succumbs to a rattlesnake bite. In the original Henry Hathaway version, Little Blackie performs the courageous river crossing with Mattie aboard, as he does in the Coen brothers' version, but the horse lives to tell the tale.

In the remake, the horses are plain saddlehorses, with only Little Blackie's bravery distinguishing him, though in the scene in which Mattie picks Little Blackie out from the group of her father's horses, she says, "This one's beautiful," and we get a close-up of his soft, gentle, noble eye. But in the original, John Wayne's horse is a dazzler. The gorgeous hunk of horseflesh is Wayne's usual make and model—chestnut with a white face and three white socks—and he knocks your eyes out. No wonder he was John Wayne's favorite; the horse is also huge and able to carry such a big man as Wayne with ease. Every scene he was in left me hypnotized by his beauty. If this was indeed the Wayne favorite, Dollor, he was an American Quarter Horse born in 1967, according to publicists. However, this would make him a yearling in 1968, when the film was being shot, and no yearling would be that large or be able to carry huge John Wayne, another clue that mendacity in the myth of Dollor is rampant and that the beloved Bo played this part. Even the original film's Little Blackie, though black of coat, flashes, with a blaze face and socks. Henry Hathaway must have wanted the fancy horses to adorn his landscape, as there are many pastoral scenes of the three amigos riding across gorgeous green fields backdropped by snowcapped mountains.

Serious, old-fashioned horsemen, in reality, prefer plainer horses, as they believe (unfoundedly) that the white feet at the end of socks are weaker than the usual black feet, and for a cowboy, the toughness of a horse's foot is essential. The horse business saying "no hoof, no horse" is considered an absolute.

I admit that I love Jeff Bridges. Seeing The Dude (from *The Big Lebowski* [1998]) on horseback thrilled me. Bridges's greasy hair and scruffy appearance make Rooster Cogburn much more realistic (the old West was a dirty place in which personal hygiene suffered) than John Wayne's seriously cleaned-up Cogburn, and one must assume that the Oscar awarded to Wayne was more of a lifetime achievement award than one for his performance in *True Grit* because he can only play one character—and that is himself, the Duke. Between The Dude and the Duke there can be no comparison, at least in my mind: Bridges is far superior, though the Duke's horse is forever ingrained in my memory.

The river crossing by Mattie and Little Blackie is a classic scene in both versions, though in the Coen brothers' remake, mechanical horses, a mechanical horse's head, and some stunt riding create the illusion. In the original, a stunt woman and a real horse complete the action, though it must be noted that it would be impossible to tell the difference. Rooster Cogburn was based on a real US marshal, a tough nut named Heck Thomas, known to be a drinking roughneck whose path often led him to violence. And that stunt at the end of the original? That is truly John Wayne jumping that fence on his horse—Wayne insisted on performing the stunt himself, forcing Henry Hathaway to shoot this scene last, just in case Wayne perished in the attempt. But this horse is not Bo—it is a trick horse named Twinkle Toes, who belonged to Wayne's stunt double in the film, Tom Gosnell. Clearly, risking both the gorgeous Bo and the star Wayne was not going to happen. But even without Wayne, the film was in the can, and Gosnell could have performed the final stunt if necessary. What an ending to the Wayne legend that would have provided!

Fort Apache (1948), *She Wore a Yellow Ribbon* (1949), and *Rio Grande* (1950)

But we must return to director John Ford, as his crowning achievement of blending man and horse was his Cavalry Trilogy, made up of *Fort Apache* (1948), *She Wore a Yellow Ribbon* (1949), and *Rio Grande* (1950), all starring John Wayne, of course. In the first and third films, he plays the same character, Kirby York, while in the second, he plays his favorite character role, Nathan Brittles, who is basically Kirby York grown old and ready for retirement. The whole John Ford acting company takes part, with Victor McLaglen, Ben Johnson, Harry Carey Jr., John Agar, Ward Bond, and enough horses to thrill Ridley Scott in his childhood western fantasies (and inspire his horse-laden historical epics later). Horses are everywhere: the troopers, of course, ride them; they pull stages and wagons and carry packs; and the Indians ride their spotted pinto ponies. All of the films' riding and stunts are amazing. Shot in Utah and Arizona, the three parts of the trilogy were filmed and produced on a tight timeline: *Fort Apache* in July through October 1947; *She Wore a Yellow Ribbon* is a testament to Ford's mastery of the genre and ability to film rapidly, usually getting scenes in a single take unless his sadism overcame his good sense and he felt like torturing one of his actors with repeated stunt takes or he was simply having one of his hissy fits with an actor (he famously punched Henry Fonda in the nose during filming of *Mister Roberts* [1955] in a fit of drunken pique). During this productive period, Ford also made *Wagon Master*, released in 1950 and filmed from November through December 1949, which originated the characters Travis (Ben Johnson) and Sandy (Harry Carey Jr.), who then appeared in *Rio Grande*. Ford stuntman Cliff Lyons was second unit director on all three, which meant that he designed and directed the horse-related scenes with a devoted group of fearless stuntmen.

The Cavalry Trilogy documents life for cavalry members in their forts and their ongoing wars with Indian tribes always in danger of coming together to defeat the white man once and for all. *She Wore a Yellow Ribbon* happens in the immediate aftermath of the rout of General George Armstrong Custer at Bull Run, and the other two are similarly dated. Though one would think fort life, except for Indian battles, would be boring and quotidian, in Fordland, good temper is exuded by the constantly singing and serenading troopers, and Ford always provides a woman for romantic interest, for either Wayne or one of Ford's young stars. Romance flourished at the forts, despite the scarcity of female beauty.

In *Fort Apache*, Kirby York is just a captain under a new commanding officer, Colonel Owen Thursday (Henry Fonda), whose vainglorious pretentiousness forces him to feel that this posting is beneath him, so he is bent on finding glory and reclaiming his famous career, even if it means the death of most of his men. He betrays York's treaty with Cochise, resulting in the slaughter of the US troops. Shirley Temple, at seventeen, plays the colonel's daughter, Philadelphia Thursday, in a bit of casting that is tremendous fun as she can pout and weep with the best of them. The film also introduced John Agar (then actually married to Shirley Temple) as Lieutenant O'Rourke, Philadelphia's love interest. The best part of the film, however, is Ben Johnson (1918–1996) and his spectacular riding as the stunt double for both Agar and Fonda. Whether as part of the classic runaway stagecoach that Ford loved so much or a race into battle, Johnson's riding is the best in movie history for me. It was during the filming of *Fort Apache* that there actually was a runaway stage, with crazed, stampeding horses and three actors in a wagon about to die as the horses seemed intent on running into a cliff wall just ahead. Johnson, who happened to be mounted and in cavalry uniform, took off on his horse Steel, caught up with the crazed horse team, and stopped it before tragedy could ensue. Ford was so grateful to the heroic Johnson that he gave him a seven-year, $5,000-a-week contract and realized that he had something special and authentic in the stuntman, who would also act and do his own stunts in the second part of the trilogy, *She Wore a Yellow Ribbon*.

In *She Wore a Yellow Ribbon*, Wayne plays a captain twenty years older than the actor was at the time and about to retire. It was shot in glorious Technicolor and won cinematographer Winton Hoch an Academy Award. Wayne felt he deserved the Oscar for playing Nathan Brittles, as it was his favorite role of his career. For me, though, it was Ben Johnson who stole the show as the ubiquitous Sergeant Travis Tyree, the most accomplished rider of the troop and, therefore, the one getting all of the most dangerous assignments of scouting territory ahead, alone, and almost always encountering bands of marauding Indians from whom he must escape. In one thrilling scene worthy of Rex the Devil Horse, Johnson rides hell-for-leather before thirty or forty Indians and ends up on a cliff, surely about to die. He says, "Come on, boy," to his horse, backs him up a few steps, and leaps from the cliff to another cliff, many feet away, something the Indians are loath to attempt. Johnson's horse Steel is a magnificent sorrel Quarter Horse with a wide blaze, three socks, and the Ben Johnson quirk of an untrimmed forelock that hangs well over his eyes as if he were a rock star; this sets Steel apart from all the other horses who sport the usual horse hairdo (and endears him to me, as I am someone who always left forelocks untrimmed). Steel is as unique and heroic as Johnson, and the rapport the two share makes them appear more centaur than man and horse. The great horse scene of the film comes when Johnson and Wayne loose all of the Indian's ponies and the horses stampede through the Indian camp. In the film, this effort was to prevent a war between the cavalry and the Indians; because Indians (according to the film's logic) find walking humiliating—as, I suspect, did Ben Johnson—they were unable to ride to meet the troops with their horses escaped.

Rio Grande features Wayne, as Colonel Kirby York, now with a mustache and soul patch, in midcareer. Travis and Sandy (Johnson and Carey) are recruits here and must perform a ridiculously dangerous stunt, Roman riding. Supposedly, the ancient Romans showed off their horsemanship skills by standing on two galloping horses, one foot on each, after having mounted by vaulting onto the horses from behind—also known as a crupper mount (perfected earlier by Yakima Canutt). Carey performs this credibly, and so does young Claude Jarman Jr.; however, Johnson is once again the star. Not only does he gallop at top speed atop the two black idiot Thoroughbreds (according to Harry Carey, who was given a more docile duo of Quarter Horses), but he takes a six-foot jump without a bobble or a care. Was there anything this man couldn't do on a horse? In *Rio Grande*, he must escape from the troop or be arrested for defending his sister's honor by killing a man, so he throws his saddle over Steel's back and mounts without girthing the saddle, such was his balance and horsemanship. This would be nearly impossible for mere mortals.

In all parts of the Cavalry Trilogy, Ford gives the horses more to do than just being cowboy-mobiles. Horses panic, rear, vocalize, stampede, and in general act like real horses instead of silent props. I'd like to think that Ford's discovery of the extent of Johnson's talents had something to do with this, as he once again (since the departure of Yakima Canutt) had a horseman worthy of his directorial talents and of his sadistic streak.

The Wild Bunch (1969) and *Pat Garrett and Billy The Kid* (1973)

When considering the Ford filmography, the anti-Ford must also be considered: Sam Peckinpah (1925–1984). In stark contrast to Ford's warmth, sentimentality, righteous codes of honor, and clear love of his characters and even their foibles, Peckinpah is a total misanthrope. He hates men (ruthless killers), women (whores), children (cruel little demons), and, seemingly, most animals, even horses. His 1969 western *The Wild Bunch* was considered revolutionary at the time for its horrific violence, but to our twenty-first-century Quentin Tarantino–ed brains, it appears tame; furthermore, even with a stellar cast, including William Holden, Robert Ryan, and Ben Johnson, it drags. The opening scene, of children torturing a scorpion, establishes a world without innocence, a world filled with evil. What follows is a spree of violent episodes that may have thrilled film critic Pauline Kael at the time and sent early viewers running for the restrooms to vomit but that has little effect now. And the horses! Though they are put through their stunt paces, completing dramatic falls (and Ben Johnson, in his sixties, can still outride anybody), they are allowed no personality or sentience. In fact, most of the horses are such plain dark-brown equines that they might belong to an industrial fleet of cars, as if Peckinpah saw them as no more than the appropriate means of travel for the time. In a nod to tradition, Peckinpah did use Yakima Canutt's sons, Joe and Tap, for stunts. He also employed as head wrangler and trainer Chema Hernandez, who is Mexico's leading horse trainer for the movies and has a filmography as long as Ben Johnson's legs. Hernandez's work is utterly stunning and impressive but without any feeling for the horses as individuals.

Pat Garret and Billy the Kid (1973) was Peckinpah's next movie after *The Wild Bunch,* and it features an excess of cool in the personages of James Coburn (with his toothy smirk and low-key delivery of lines), Kris Kristofferson, Bob Dylan (who also wrote songs for the film, including "Knockin' on Heaven's Door"), and Harry Dean Stanton. Filmed entirely in Durango, Mexico, this film must have been one fun set to visit, especially with the director's and Coburn's reputedly epic drinking; one can only imagine the drug abuse and partying in the isolated setting. However, it too seems limp and underimagined, lacking in likable characters, although I suspect we're supposed to like Billy (Kristofferson), even though he's a cold-blooded murderer. Kristofferson is not an actor who can pull this off. And once again, the horses are utilized for mind-numbing stunts (one wonders if, in Mexico, the Humane Society monitored cruelty to horses at that time) by the ubiquitous Chema Hernandez. One horse does a complete somersault forward; that the rider didn't die is incredible.

A bit of warmth and humanity could have been injected into both these Peckinpah films if the horses were given personalities and valued by their characters/riders. But such depiction is outside of Peckinpah's wheelhouse. Without empathy and compassion, Bloody Sam (as he came to be called after *The Wild Bunch*) was rumored to be an alcoholic and cocaine addict and, I assume from his reputed addictions, a total narcissist interested only in his own needs who had no interest in horses, though they are the vehicle defining the western.

Wagon Master (1950)

I've saved the details of the very best for last: Ben Johnson (1918–1996). Primarily a stuntman and bit performer for John Ford and Sam Peckinpah, Johnson was that rare thing in Hollywood, the real deal. A world champion rodeo performer like his father, Johnson was riding horses before he could walk on his father's horse and cattle ranch in Oklahoma. In 1940, he drove a trailer full of horses to the Arizona set of *The Outlaw* (1943) and did some training and stunt work for about a week (as well as acting in an uncredited role as a deputy), for which he received a check for $300. As a working cowboy making a dollar a day on his father's ranch, he decided Hollywood was for him. Johnson made hundreds of movies and television shows, as an actor, stuntman, and wrangler, but his films for Ford, frequently with John Wayne, cemented his career. Of Irish and Cherokee descent, Johnson makes one suspect that riding ability can be, at least partially, genetic.

To understand the miracle that occurred when Ben Johnson was on a horse, one must watch John Ford's 1950 film *Wagon Master*. The film starred Johnson and his good friend and another Ford regular, Harry Carey Jr., as horse traders who take jobs guiding a wagon train of Mormons (by chance, Carey's own horse was named Mormon, and he rode him in the film) to their new home in a fertile valley. In this film, Johnson rode his own horse Steel, that beautiful sorrel Quarter Horse with a wide blaze, four socks, and handsome, long forelock. Clearly, Johnson and Steel had a profound rapport, and

Johnson could do anything with this horse—well, actually, with any horse. Johnson was, by far, the best rider ever in westerns, completely one with his horse, unmoving in the saddle, his long legs in stirrups nearly to the ground (he was six feet two and could mount his little Quarter Horse just by swinging one long leg over). He became a part of the horse rather than a rider of the horse. Harry Carey Jr., whose father had been a cowboy star himself, had been riding since childhood as well, but Johnson makes him look like an amateur.

Wagon Master features several scenes in which Johnson gets to show off his riding skill, though showing off was simply not a part of his easygoing personality. He just can't help himself. In the river crossing sequence, in which Johnson and Carey shepherd the wagon train through the water, Travis (Johnson) is everywhere with Steel, leading frightened pulling horses, checking on all the wagons, and testing out the waters ahead, utterly fearless. A particularly nice touch is the foal crossing with his mother. But Travis is the star here.

Then there's the bucking scene, in which gunshots are supposed to rile Travis's horse into prolonged bucking. John Ford's sadistic sense of humor made the scene what it was, because it was said you could set off a firecracker under Steel, to no effect. Unbeknownst to Johnson, Ford had another crew member bring in a rodeo bucking bronco and made the horse up to look like Steel. It's impossible to imagine that Johnson didn't recognize that this was a ringer, but affable Johnson did whatever the Old Man told him to do; he got on the horse and proceeded to stick to him like glue through manic bucking. No double was used here: Johnson did all his own stunts. At the end of the scene, Johnson was supposed to fall off the horse—an unprecedented event as no horse could throw Johnson—which he did, hitting the dirt hard, and got up. Ford, famed for doing scenes in one take, announced that Johnson and the bronco had gotten out of the camera's frame briefly, so he needed it to be done again. One doubts the veracity of the director's claim, knowing his evil sense of humor and desire to torment his actors when he pleased.

But Johnson did the scene again, stuck to the horse, hit the dirt hard, and once again got up and dusted himself off.

In another scene, the wagon train reaches a river, having gone miles and miles without water, and the horses and humans are delighted, drinking, thrashing, bathing. Johnson unsaddles and unbridles Steel and then effortlessly swings himself up on the naked horse, bareback, with just a hunk of mane in one hand. Having ridden bareback and, like a mortal, needing to be helped to get on board, I found this godlike lack of effort astonishing.

The horses in *Wagon Master* have more personality than those in most Ford films, as they vocalize constantly, snort, and shake their heads. But Steel just has to be Steel, and frankly, Johnson just has to be Johnson. He is a natural actor as well as a horseman, and he won the 1972 Oscar for Best Supporting Actor for his work in *The Last Picture Show*, along with just about every other award for this character on the planet. In 1971, most of the world may not have been aware of him as an actor, but horse aficionados knew him well as a horseman without equal.

John Wayne is a good rider; however, he rides like he walks, heavily, and of course, a star of his magnitude couldn't be risked doing his own stunts. Ben Johnson, however, rides with a preternatural lightness and lack of effort that, to anyone who has ever ridden, is a joy to behold. I like Wayne now, though earlier in life I couldn't forgive him for his politics, and I appreciate the way in which he came to embody the western in films. But here I must admit: I am in love with Ben Johnson. He famously said, "I may not be much of an actor, but I can play Ben Johnson better than anybody else."

4

A Day at the Races

Broadway Bill (1934) and Riding High (1950)

Hollywood has long had a love affair with horse racing. Bing Crosby owned Del Mar Racetrack in San Diego County and thrilled fans by taking tickets at the door and making regular appearances with his many famous friends. Numerous other stars got bitten by the racing bug and even more by the gambling bug. I myself, as a child, saw Cary Grant at Hollywood Park, a sighting I'll never forget. Who has more disposable income than movie people? So movies about horse racing abounded in the golden age of Hollywood, the 1930s, and some of them feature iconic, sentient horses who are unforgettable. Hollywood royalty, like Frank Capra, made and remade horse racing films.

Frank Capra (1897–1991) was surely a workaholic. In 1934 alone, he had released his masterpiece, *It Happened One Night*, which cleaned up at the Oscars, as it should have. A comedy about a runaway heiress and the journalist on her trail, starring Claudette Colbert and Clark Gable, it retains its charm and its delightful risqueness, which features Clark Gable removing his shirt to demonstrate his contempt for undershirts, a blow to the men's underwear industry, which sank by 75 percent after the film's release. Later that year, Capra released his racetrack film, *Broadway Bill*, retooling the runaway heiress part for Myrna Loy (clearly Capra had a penchant for leading ladies with witty, unconventionally beautiful faces like Colbert and Loy; others from that same era include Carole Lombard and Barbara Stanwyck, all of whom simply look smart and full of fun). Capra wanted Clark Gable for the male lead; what a pleasure it would have been to see him develop his wise-ass chemistry seen in *It Happened One Night* opposite Loy. But Gable was otherwise employed, so Capra settled for the charisma-free, wit-free Warner Baxter, an actor who was terrified of horses, much to Capra's chagrin. Loy, on the other hand, has many deeply caring scenes with the eponymous horse Broadway Bill. But Capra yearned to remake the film with a hero who was truly a horse lover and did in 1950, with Bing Crosby as his star. Bing Crosby, as mentioned, loved racing, the racetrack, and horses, but the resultant film, *Riding High*, was a failure at the box office and with critics. In 1934, Myrna Loy's career was about to skyrocket, as it was also the year in which her best character, Nora Charles, was introduced in the first of the Thin Man movies. Nora was sophisticated, smart, and witty and quite a sleuth to boot, a paean to clever casting that to this day reflects Loy's great chemistry with William Powell as Nick Charles, who is an equally charming and sophisticated sleuth (plus, they had a great dog, the wire-haired fox terrier Asta).

The titular horse, Broadway Bill, has far more charm and personality than Warner Baxter, and though no trainer is credited in the film, whoever trained Bill did a great job. Bill is quirky as hell. He will only get in the gate and run if he has, at his barn, the companionship of his beloved rooster, Skeeter, who rides on his back when training and whom the horse grooms with love. Myrna Loy speaks to him, and he understands her and even gets up from near death for her. His willingness to lay down and play sick, baring his teeth and breathing heavily, make him far more interesting than Baxter, whose line delivery has no snap or crackle to it.

The film begins with a family dinner for the extremely dull, extremely wealthy Higgins clan, of which Alice (Myrna Loy) is the youngest of four daughters and the only one unmarried. The eldest daughter, Margaret, is married to Dan Brooks (Baxter), a former racehorse trainer with a dubious past. Each of the elder Higgins sons-in-law have had bestowed on them a sinecure, running one of Mr. Higgins's boring businesses; Dan Brooks runs the long-established Higgins cardboard box factory without enthusiasm, and sales are way down due to his lack of management skills. At the family dinner/meeting, Mr. Higgins dresses down Brooks for his shoddy work, and Brooks just quits, walks out on the Higgins family and on his wife. He owns a very fast horse, Broadway Bill, and longs to get him to the track.

There is an attraction between Brooks and his young sister-in-law, as she is the only Higgins with spirit and interests outside the family's businesses and wealth. When he peremptorily leaves with Broadway Bill and nary a penny to his name, Alice (whom he calls Princess) comes to his and Bill's rescue, showing up at the racetrack with Skeeter and demonstrating her willingness to do whatever racetrack work Brooks requires. She even sells her jewelry to provide the money Brooks needs to enter Bill into the Imperial Derby.

The racetrack setting resembles a real racetrack with all its foibles, including tampering with odds, bribing jockeys, and attempts to fix races, but Dan and Alice live in a fairy tale racetrack world, with a clean horse and derby dreams. Unfortunately, a rival owner bribes a jockey to ride Bill poorly. Dan warns the jockey not to hold Bill back, as he has plenty of both speed and stamina, so of course, in the derby, his jockey fights the horse and holds him back as much as he can. Still, the horse has such great heart that he pulls to the lead and wins the race, only to drop dead just past the finish line. The attending vet says, "His heart just burst."

Bill appears to be a handsome chestnut, with a star, strip, and snip on his noble face, and his humanlike emotions are never in doubt. Indeed, Dan and Alice treat him as their child (another family member is Dan's exercise rider and stable hand, Whitey, played by the great character actor Clarence Muse, an African American subjected to none of the racist clichés in movies at the time), and through Bill, it's clear that Dan and Alice are meant for each other. Bill further demonstrates his acting ability in a terrible thunderstorm, when he vocalizes, rears, and appears terrified. Because of the leaky roof in his stall, he catches pneumonia, causing the touching scenes between the horse and Alice. Alice, as she must, returns to her musty home. When Dan comes to the Higgins house to spirit Alice away, he has, in tow, Whitey (of course) but also two new horses: Broadway Bill II and Princess.

Broadway Bill didn't come close to the financial and critical success of *It Happened One Night*, with the former taking in box office sales of $1.4 million compared to the latter's $2.5 million, nor does it have the ribald charm and wit of the latter. But unlike *It Happened One Night*, it has a horse who can act, who outshines the film's leading man, and who competes with Loy for lovableness and wit.

A Day at the Races (1937) and *Stablemates* (1938)

Filmed at Santa Anita Racetrack and the back lot of MGM in Culver City, California, *A Day at the Races* (1937) stands out as an anomaly in film in general. Starring the Marx brothers, it is an hour and a half of nearly unplotted chaos that features a surprisingly knowledgeable racehorse, Hi Hat. Directed by Sam Wood (1883–1949), who also directed *A Night at the Opera* (1935) with the Marx brothers, this seems a film in search of a director because all Wood does is point the camera at the various vaudeville sketches and musical numbers that make up the film while letting Groucho, Chico, and Harpo display their ridiculous hilarity. Though no record of any horse trainer seems to exist, an ex-jockey named Danny Montrose was an uncredited technical adviser for the horse racing scenes, and there is, in Groucho's autobiography, a hint that journeyman assistant director at MGM Al Shenberg, though also uncredited, was in charge of the racing scenes. Shenberg was also an assistant on such films as *I Am a Fugitive from a Chain Gang* (1932) and *The Wizard of Oz* (1939) and was the nephew of MGM honcho Louis B. Mayer, a known horse racing aficionado. Shenberg seems a natural choice as someone who could bring some rationality to the horse racing milieu, complete with African American stable, or "back side," workers, a staple of track life in the early twentieth century.

The putative plot concerns Judy (Maureen O'Sullivan), a young woman who owns a financially struggling sanatorium in a Saratoga-like setting, complete with racetrack. The evil Mr. Morgan wants to repossess the sanatorium and turn it into a casino. The sanatorium has one good client, Mrs. Upjohn (Groucho's frequent foil, Margaret Dumont), who seems about to leave to seek out the attentions of a Florida doctor, Hugo Z. Hackenbush, the only one who understands her imaginary maladies. Dr. Hackenbush (Groucho), we discover, is actually a horse veterinarian who has hornswoggled Mrs. Upjohn into believing he is a real doctor. Judy's employee, Tony (Chico), has the big idea to hire Dr. Hackenbush to come work at the sanatorium, thereby retaining Mrs. Upjohn as a client and perhaps getting a loan from her to pay off Judy's mortgage. Meanwhile, Judy's boyfriend has bought a racehorse that he believes will win and pay off Judy's mortgage. The boyfriend, a singer, is also Hi Hat's trainer, and his exercise rider and jockey is Stuffy (Harpo), who actually seems able to ride quite well (his shoulder was injured during shooting, causing a delay, when he was bucked off a Shetland pony).

Hi Hat's utter hatred of his previous owner, the aforementioned Morgan, provides the impetus for much of the plot. He goes berserk when he sees Morgan and tries to kill him; during the race finale, all Stuffy has to do to urge the horse on is show him a photo of Morgan, and Hackenbush machinates to get Morgan's voice on the racetrack loudspeaker to also spur Hi Hat on. Stuffy communicates with and kisses Hi Hat, and early on, at his veterinary office, Hackeenbush talks to a horse patient, who talks back. In this zany world, horses are every bit as smart as humans.

It's discovered that Hi Hat is a slow nag as a racehorse, but during one escape-from-Morgan scene, he demonstrates serious jumping ability, clearing an automobile and multiple obstacles with ease, making him a sure thing as a steeplechase horse. Entered into a steeplechase stakes race, with Stuffy as jockey, his main rival is ridden by Frankie Darro, who also appeared in *Broadway Bill* and numerous Rex the Devil Horse serials, among other films. Darro grew up in a circus acrobatic family, and his small size and athletic prowess and fearlessness made him able to play teenaged characters well into his twenties and, of course, to play jockeys. After a fall into a muddy pool, the riders somehow switch horses, and it is revealed that Hi Hat actually won, though he was ridden by Darro to the finish line; Judy's sanatorium is saved. It does appear that Stuffy does much of the actual riding (Hi Hat also is ridden by both Harpo and Chico and eventually joined by Groucho in some scenes), though certainly putting Stuffy's curly wig on any rider would make the jockey in the racing scenes difficult to determine.

This all makes *A Day at the Races* sound much more linear than it really is. For no reason, musical numbers appear out of nowhere to stop the action completely, and scenes of Groucho playing doctor also cause the plot to cease, though they are a delight. When Groucho examines Harpo, taking his pulse, he says, "Either he's dead or my watch has stopped," as only he can deliver a line. There is likewise a hilarious scene of Groucho examining Mrs. Upjohn. The film is actually all about the schtick of the Marx brothers, who took the screenplay on a vaudeville tour before filming, perfecting the jokes and cutting and adding scenes until they felt it was ready to be filmed.

For horse lovers, though, this is a film about Hi Hat, a horse who loves, hates, jumps, and carts around all three Marx brothers with ease. He is a real trooper, willing to hide in hotel rooms, in ambulances, and wherever else the brothers want him to stay. There is no data available about who Hi Hat really was, though he does appear to be a Thoroughbred and an actor. The affinity that the Marx brothers have with horses seems to be one of the only realistic aspects of this film, as they demonstrate no compunctions or fears and climb on without reserve and without pausing their joking. Hi Hat becomes the fourth Marx brother here, willing to do whatever it takes to complete the chaos of the film. There's even a scene in which Harpo is slicing open a hotel room's mattress to find straw to feed Hi Hat, whose impoverished owner can't afford feed. Who would've guessed that the Marx brothers were horse lovers?

Directed by the same Sam Wood, with Al Shenberg again as second unit director and assistant director, is the 1938 film *Stablemates*, with a horse movie's favorite short guy, Mickey Rooney, only eighteen at the time of the filming, and Wallace Beery reprising a version of his role from *The Champ* (1931), though in this film he is a down-on-his-luck, alcoholic veterinarian with a sketchy past and a truculent personality. Once again, a lot of the action takes place at a racetrack, and it was filmed primarily at the now defunct Hollywood Park (though Santa Anita Racetrack and Del Mar Racetrack stood in for Hollywood when it was unavailable). Like *A Day at the Races*, the rest of the action took place on the MGM back lot in Culver City, California.

The washed-up vet, Tom Terry, and the orphaned stable boy, Mickey (the character's actual name, for a little verisimilitude), bond over a wonderful horse, Lady Q, a beautiful bay with a star, low socks, and knowing eyes, and Mickey talks to her, kisses her, appeals to her, and loves her, and she loves him back—when he goes off on a mission, she nickers after him pathetically, clearly saying goodbye in horse talk. At one point, Tom sings to her, an alarming event that scares her, which she displays by widening her eyes and nickering at him to stop. Mickey ends up owning Lady Q when her villainous owner, fed up with her lack of production on the track, wants to send her to the proverbial glue factory.

The owner, Mr. Gayle, gives her to Mickey, and when the vagrant, homeless ex-vet chooses Lady Q's stall to bed down in, he instantly recognizes that she is lame in a front foot, and believes this is due to a tumor in the hoof, a diagnosis he made in his distant past for a famous racehorse. He operated on this horse, cut out the tumor, and the horse returned to his former success. Mickey begs Tom to do the operation on Lady Q, despite his alcoholism and long-lost profession, and eventually, Tom is persuaded by Mickey's sincere adoration of the filly, and by affection for this boy who has nothing in the world except for Lady Q.

Tom, who still has his set of vet tools, says that a portion of the hoof wall must be removed so he can get to the tumor and cut it out, a delicate operation that must be performed without damaging a nerve. Eureka! Equine podiatry is invented! I was lucky enough to work for a year for the brilliant man who really invented equine podiatry, Dr. Ric Redden, who singlehandedly altered the way vets treated hoof issues in horses, and I both witnessed and helped out in numerous surgeries that demanded the removal of some hoof wall, usually due to the pressure of laminitis. Unlike in the film, it was a bloody procedure, but the alternative for a horse with laminitis, the swelling of the tissue inside the hoof wall, was euthanasia. Working with Doc Redden at his clinic in Versailles, Kentucky, was like a crash course in horse feet, and what I learned in this course was irreplaceable knowledge about dealing with hoof issues. Doc Redden is a polarizing figure in the horse business—mostly because he is always ahead of his time in his innovations and he can be ornery as a mad rhino—but because I was a hard worker and up for anything he needed help with, he and I had a wonderful relationship. The hoof wall removal in *Stablemates* is a bloodless affair and so completely unrealistic; however, the tumor is removed, without even an X-ray to determine whether it existed, and Lady Q lives to race again.

Lady Q is unique in horse film history, as her stunt double for the big race finale is none other than Seabiscuit, running in the 1938 Hollywood Gold Cup and winning handily. Never did a horse have such a stellar double. We also meet Seabiscuit, in his stall, when Mickey, by chance, hooks up with a posh lady trainer who takes him and Lady Q in. The presence of Al Shenberg ensures that the racetrack scenes are realistic, both on the front and back side (again the presence of African American stable or back side workers occurs), and a number of jockeys were uncredited advisers: Bart Tatum, Lyle Brown, Jackie Howard, Clyde Kennedy, Ed Kelly and Bill Gaffney, hardly household names, but one must assume they added to the realism of the race track scenes. And then there's Mickey Rooney, utterly fearless around horses, a complete natural with them. He clearly loved them, and they knew it and responded in kind. Perhaps this is a clue to the nature of finding sentience in horses. If you can open your heart to them and show them only affection and no fear, they will open their hearts to you. The relationship between Mickey and Lady Q is beautiful enough to cure the cantankerous ex-veterinarian of both his alcoholism and his seeming inability to love anyone, even himself. If this film sounds maudlin, it absolutely is. But it's also heartwarming, especially to this horse lover with a background in equine podiatry.

Secretariat (2010) and *Seabiscuit* (2003)

The horse racing movie made a comeback in the late twentieth and early twenty-first centuries, no doubt due to a plethora of brilliant horses with amazing careers and to a couple of truly wonderful books about these horses that begged to become movies. Such horses as Secretariat, Seabiscuit, Phar Lap, and others absolutely deserved their own movies.

A confession: Secretariat was the first horse I fell madly in love with. As a racehorse, his magnificence was unequaled. Because of his personality and greatness, a film about him was inevitable, and the 2010 film *Secretariat* does him some justice. His thirty-one-length Belmont Stakes win may be the most impressive horse race ever run. He demolished a first-class field of contenders, making them look like nags as he flew ahead of them, seemingly effortlessly. And that epic race call by Chic Anderson: "Secretariat is moving like a tremendous machine." He was gorgeous, that new penny chestnut coat, that intelligent head. He seemed to have a self-image, to know what a star he was, and legend has it that he would pose for cameras, turning toward the clicking and flashing bulbs like John Barrymore showing his fabled profile. I adored him, and it's one of the great sadnesses of my life that I didn't get to see him in the flesh, as he died before I ever made it to Kentucky, though I have visited his stall at Claiborne Farm, where his nameplate still graces the stall door, and his grave there. So how could I not love a movie dedicated to him?

As usual, the factual discrepancies in a film not thoroughly researched or interested in truth aggravate the hell out of me. Loved the horse, didn't love the movie. For the sake of drama, Penny Chenery Tweedy's winning of the Kentucky Derby with her fine gray horse Riva Ridge the year before Secretariat's win disappears from the narrative, which would have dispensed with the money trouble that might have caused her to lose her farm should Secretariat not have panned out. For the film's narrative, Secretariat has to be her only horse and her only huge winner. This is a shame, as Mrs. Tweedy was one hell of a horsewoman, especially in the early 1970s, a time when horseracing was still very much a man's game. Women trainers, riders, and even owners simply didn't exist in this tough milieu. Women were not even allowed in Kentucky breeding sheds at that time, as it was considered unseemly for women to view horses having sex. In both the film and real history, Mrs. Tweedy lives with her family in Colorado in bourgeois splendor and keeps her horses in Virginia, on her family farm. One night, her farm manager calls and says Somethingroyal, her prized mare, is approaching foaling, and she should get right down there if she wants to see the baby born.

I have foaled innumerable mares, and there is absolutely no way anyone can say that a mare is about to foal until her water breaks. And once that happens, you usually only have to wait minutes. It is utterly unpredictable. Of course, you can estimate by counting back 342 days to the date of ovulation after breeding, and you can watch the mare's udder to see if it is filling with milk. But mares may be a month early or a month late. They may wax—that is, release their first thick milk (colostrum)—for a day or for a week, or they may not wax at all (learning this nearly ruined my life, as I then realized there was no sleep in the cards for me whenever a mare neared her due date). When my vet told me that only 50 percent of mares wax, I considered suicide. There is no surefire sign that a mare is about to foal that night. Plus, mares love to foal in the middle of the night—supposedly a sound strategy as the foal is up and able to run with the herd by daybreak, but I believe this actually has to do with the mean sense of humor most mares have. So Diane Lane, as Mrs. Tweedy, puts her kids in her station wagon, rides out to the farm (Colorado to Virginia in less than a day?), and sits on a hay bale, perky as can be, watching the very polite, on-time mare foal her champion as soon as they arrive. Trainer Lucien Lauren is there too, having gotten the same phone call and teleported himself from New York. All I can say, as someone who has gone without sleep for a month waiting on an overdue mare, is this: if only.

In the film, much drama is built around an important coin toss to determine the owner of Secretariat. In this version of the story, two Chenery mares, Somethingroyal and Hasty Matelda, have been bred using a foal share with Claiborne Farm. To decide who gets which of the two foals who were born, Bull Hancock, master of Claiborne Farm, and Mrs. Tweedy toss a coin (it would have been Hancock and Christopher Chenery, Penny Chenery Tweedy's father, but Chenery had already passed away). Hancock wins the coin toss but takes the latter mare's foal, leaving Mrs. Tweedy with Somethingroyal and her 1970 foal, who would grow up to be perhaps the greatest racehorse of all time. This was decided the year before, when both mares became pregnant. Bad choice, Hancock.

The movie is based on the book *Secretariat* (1975) by much-honored turf writer William Nack, and the issues that arise with the movie don't trouble the book. Nack knows horses and racing and writes a factual account of this glorious horse's life. The coin toss so vital to the plot isn't in reality a one-off but, instead, happens every two years. Secretariat's father, leading sire Bold Ruler, was owned by an elderly widow who didn't need money from stud fees. Instead, she opted for deals with the owners of the best mares in the world, putting up the stud while the other put up the mares. She had such a deal with Christopher Chenery, so the matter of who would own the foal who grew up to be Secretariat was really settled the year before. As well, Riva Ridge, Chenery's color-bearer who was three years old in 1972, won that year's Kentucky Derby, cementing a year in which the Chenerys' farm, Meadows Stable, won over a million dollars. The Chenerys were rich. But once Christopher Chenery died, the inheritance tax on his massive fortune amounted to over ten million dollars, precipitating a financial crisis during Secretariat's two-year-old year and forcing Mrs. Tweedy to consider syndicating him as a three-year-old, as long as she retained the right to race him as she saw fit.

But the racing is glorious. Head wrangler, stunt coordinator, and second unit director Rusty Hendrickson selected five horses to play the great Big Red, one of those from an open casting call at the 2009 Secretariat Festival at the Bourbon County, Kentucky, Fairgrounds' "Look Alike Contest," where Hendrickson and fellow judges Secretariat jockey Ron Turcotte and two exercise riders from Meadows Stable, picked a winner. Mechanical Secretariats were also used for some close-up shots for verisimilitude. The errors omnipresent in the farm part of the film don't exist in the racing part, and Secretariat's Triple Crown victories remain thrilling, as does the eponymous horse himself, a big, lovable teddy bear who adores his owner; his groom from childhood, Eddie Sweat; and his worshipful public. Director Randall Wallace, best known for writing the screenplay for *Braveheart* (1995), makes Secretariat a real character, with eerily human eyes and an ability to communicate with the humans he loves. He vocalizes frequently and turns his lordly head toward clicking cameras with grace. Races are re-created with fastidious attention to detail, and even though I knew Secretariat won and won, tension is created as you root for Big Red with all your heart, despite the horse lore flaws that abound.

The gold standard of horse racing movies, however, is *Seabiscuit* (2003), based on the fastidiously researched, elegantly written book

Seabiscuit, 2003. Race day for the Biscuit, with Tobey Maguire up, Chris Cooper, and Jeff Bridges. (Universal Pictures/Dreamworks/Photofest. ©Universal Pictures/ Dreamworks. Photographer: Francois Duhamel.)

of the same name by Laura Hillenbrand, who remains an outspoken supporter of racehorses to this day. First, what the hell is a Seabiscuit? One needs to examine the horse's pedigree superficially to see that his sire was a son of Man o' War named Hard Tack. And what the hell is Hard Tack? It is a dry, flat bread packed by cowboys going out on the trail, because it lasts forever. Seabiscuit is simply another name for it, though it is likewise another name for the round, flat creature known as a Sand Dollar, because of its resemblance to a silver dollar. Mystery solved.

The Biscuit is a small (fifteen hands), plain, brown Thorough-bred, with a huge personality (to the point that there is a credited "horse vocalizer" named Gary Hecker responsible for the Biscuit's frequent commentary on his life) and a darling little head, com-plete with the requisite soulful eyes. Like Secretariat, he has roots at legendary Claiborne Farm, in Kentucky, but is underappreciated there, and his first trainer, Sunny Jim Fitzsimmons, unaware of his potential, treats him like a nag, beating and enraging the poor horse. The rap on the Biscuit, from foalhood, is that he's lazy, sleeps all the time, and eats too much. In the film world, this may be a detriment, but it is different in the real world. I worked with a trainer who'd trained a world champion American Quarter Horse that slept all the time and ate vast amounts, and my trainer acknowledged that this was the sign of an intelligent horse saving himself for when it mattered: race day.

Luckily, a horse whisperer and trainer, Tom Smith (Chris Cooper), sees something special in the wounded spirit of this horse and enlists a fearless jockey, Red Pollard (Tobey Maguire), to help reclaim him. Pollard, like the Biscuit, is a wounded soul filled with anger, and horse and rider are twinned, just as the trajectory of the story is mated with the nation's falling into the Great Depression and then bravely, with fine leadership, exiting it. Like Franklin Delano Roosevelt, owner of Seabiscuit Charles Howard (Jeff Bridges) is a self-made man whose faith in his horse and his horse's people remains unshakable, and he is at the heart of the inspiration for Seabiscuit's success. As are the horses in *Secretariat*, the Biscuit is given humanlike characteristics and seems to be in love with his owner, trainer, and rider as well as his companion, the gorgeous palomino pal who shares his stall and provides him with equine friendship for the first time, Pumpkin. Some sixty horses were used in the making of this film, as well as mechanical horses and horses' heads, and the same head wrangler, Rusty Hendrickson, was responsible for the horses. We can begin to see the Rusty Hendrickson worldview: horses are intelligent, loving beings, bad only when mistreated by humans, attached as cocker spaniels to their owners. The apotheosis of this will be evident in *Dances with Wolves*, another Hendrickson vehicle.

Seabiscuit the movie is enhanced by the presence of Hall of Fame jockey Gary Stevens playing the famous jockey George "The Iceman" Woolf and by races designed by another Hall of Famer, Chris McCarron, who also appears as Charlie Kurtsinger, the jockey of Seabiscuit's cross-country nemesis War Admiral. Love of racing and dedication to accurate reconstruction of races is evident in every scene, giving this film a heightened reality lacking in at least half of *Secretariat*; plus, there is the thrill, for racing fans, of seeing two such eternal favorites as Stevens and McCarron on screen. In reality, Seabiscuit and War Admiral were related: War Admiral's father and Seabiscuit's grandfather were the same original Big Red, Man o' War, making the Biscuit War Admiral's nephew.

Shortly after Red Pollard breaks his leg in a riding accident, the Biscuit ruptures a tendon (although not before having as his substitute rider Woolf, who, coached by Pollard, beats War Admiral, a huge seventeen-hand black beast, in that famous match race); they convalesce together and cement their friendship even more. Like Mrs. Tweedy, Pollard talks to the Biscuit as if he were a human, providing both with the companionship and family they had lost early in life (both are brutally weaned). Having had meaningful conversations with many horses myself, including one with a mare of whom I could ask a question ("Where does it hurt?") and expect an answer (nose to heel bulb, where indeed an abscess was forming), I know only too well how satisfying talking to horses can be.

In reality, Seabiscuit had a record of eighty-nine starts, thirty-three wins, fifteen seconds, and thirteen thirds, for total earnings of $419,265 for Charles Howard, and was retired to an undistinguished stud career after racing. But there can be no question that, like Secretariat, he inherited an enormous heart from his dam, both literally and figuratively (the huge heart gene can only be passed down from the dam, not from the sire, part of which made Secretariat such a magnificent broodmare sire). With no glaring horse-related errors, *Seabiscuit* provides us with a horse hero to adore.

50 to 1 (2014)

No racing fan will ever forget the 2009 Kentucky Derby, in which Mine That Bird, a 50–1 long shot, came from far off the pace to win, in a signature rail-skimming ride from the fearless Calvin Borel (nicknamed Calvin Bo-Rail). The brown gelding was already a big story, as his connections weren't the usual international bluebloods but were instead a Quarter Horse owner from New Mexico and a small-time trainer at Sunland Park, and Mine That Bird's transportation to the Derby, instead of being a Lear jet, was a beat-up horse trailer that made the endless trek from New Mexico to Kentucky, the trainer, with his recently broken leg, doing the driving. I remember that the race caller had a moment of utter confusion, when he had no idea who the horse striking the front was.

The movie *50 to 1* (2014) is a trifle, directed and cowritten by *Dances with Wolves* producer Jim Wilson, with some seriously poor human acting (the biggest names on board are William Devane and Skeet Ulrich), but the horse who plays Bird is sensational. He is of course a dead ringer for the original Bird, a small, plain brown colt with a little star on his forehead, but from the first time we glimpse him, he has personality. Bird gets out of stalls by himself and has adventures, refuses to be caught once loose, nods in agreement when his humans talk to him, loves to eat donuts with sprinkles, takes his groom's hat over and over, and paws the ground and nods when he acknowledges that he's ready to race. The fact that trainer Chip Woolley can engage in conversation with him, and expect a response, is taken for granted.

Mine That Bird was by an undistinguished sire from heiress Mary Lou Whitney's breeding program, Birdstone, and only brought $9,500 as a yearling but made a name for himself winning stakes races at two in Canada. And he was very small—being a May baby didn't help his prospects at the sale, though he had a nice pedigree featuring inbreeding to Mr. Prospector, Northern Dancer, and Bold Ruler. Privately purchased as a two-year-old by New Mexican Mark Allen and well-known New Mexico veterinarian Leonard Blach, the colt ended up in Woolley's care because of a chance meeting with the new owner Allen at a bar fight. The best part of the movie is in the clever editing, using footage from Mine That Bird's actual Derby win with the newly shot action to create fabulous verisimilitude. And the coup de grâce: getting Calvin Borel to play himself. People who follow Kentucky racing love Borel for his dauntless riding of the rail, putting to good use the cliché that the shortest distance between two points is a straight line. Borel is known for saving ground and being unafraid to get his mount right up against the rail, through tiny holes between other horses. This heightens the realistic feel to the film, as scripted scenes with Borel are perfectly mated with Borel at the actual Derby.

Films about underdogs are innately successful, and the class gap between the cowboy-hatted Mine That Bird team and the riches and royalty of all the other Derby contenders' teams is the overwhelming theme of this film. Bird himself is tiny and an underdog. His trainer is about to go bankrupt. His sire never made the big time. But the little guy could run; ultimately, racing isn't a beauty contest, nor does it obey the rules of nature. Bird himself points out how achievement can come from anywhere, even Sunland Park Racetrack in New Mexico.

The movie *50 to 1* suffers from some outlandish slapstick indicating the fecklessness of the humans and features one glaring mistake: when Woolley assesses the colt from the side and says, "He's a little crooked up front." As a veteran of horse sales in the position of owner/buyer/seller and agent, I know that crookedness must first be assessed from a head-on view, where one can easily note feet that turn in or out, or by observing the horse walk toward you and identifying a bad, clumsy gait and unforgiveable knees. But that is quickly forgiven, as Bird himself is so damned cute and smart. Only Borel can harness the speed and tenacity of that colt—the perfect jockey for a come-from-behind runner, and he too talks to the colt during the running of the Derby, telling him when it's time to run. Aside from Bird's performance, the only other reason to watch this film is for its scathing portrayal of leading trainer Bob Baffert as a supercilious, sarcastic big mouth. Bird's antics when free are the best part of the film, and Bill Lawrence, listed as "liberty horse trainer," is responsible; he gave the intelligent horse visual cues from outside the camera's sight, and Bird's childlike mischief is a delight.

Dark Horse (2015)

The Welsh village of Cefn Fforest died when the coal mines that employed nearly all of its inhabitants were shut down, and the remaining population are pasty, gray, older, overweight, tattooed, and in a perpetual state of hopelessness. All of the young people seem to have vanished, no doubt headed to London or other cities where employment is possible and dreams abound. There are no dreams left in Cefn Fforest, until the barmaid at the Working Men's Club, the local pub that features "old time dancing" and ale, gets an idea. The film *Dark Horse* (2015), directed by New Zealander James Napier Robertson (1982–), depicts the crux of this idea in the shape of a single horse, Dream Alliance, who won the Welsh National Cup in steeple chasing, and in so doing restored hope and community to the village. The documentary won all of New Zealand's awards for which it was eligible and was declared "the greatest film made in New Zealand."

Janet Vokes, who bred budgies and whippets as a girl, worked in a factory for twenty-three years to support her family but when the documentary opens is a waitress, serving drinks to a local accountant who is known to have had racehorses. Vokes has the dream of breeding and owning a Thoroughbred racehorse. Her husband was a junk man, with a horse and buggy, who rode through the streets of the village shouting "rags, bones, iron," and she sometimes rode with him and liked his horse. Why not breed and own a racehorse? The fact that such notables as the queen of England, the king of Dubai, and other rich folk and members of high society make up the racehorse ownership in Great Britain doesn't deter her (a similar theme as that in *50 to 1*). She cajoles the accountant, who has sworn to his wife that he will lose no more money on racehorses, until he gives in and agrees to create and manage a syndicate of ownership. Then Janet convinces twenty-three village inhabitants to put in ten pounds a week to jump start this dream.

Mrs. Vokes has steely will and determination, and mischief in her eyes. She takes a second job, as a janitor (or "cleaner," as she calls herself) at the local supermarket to be able to afford her share and sets about asking everyone she knows about how she might buy a Thoroughbred mare. She finally finds a young man who has an utterly nondescript mare for sale for a thousand pounds. She and the mister go to look at the mare, who raced three times and finished last in one race and was pulled up (stopped before the finish line) in the others. The mare, Rewbell, has scarred legs from unpleasant encounters with fences and other impediments on the farm. Mr. Vokes tells the young man that she isn't worth a thousand pounds and offers three hundred, which the owner accepts. Now the syndicate has a mare.

Of course, they can't afford the high stud fees that the best stallions get. As an alternative they pick a stud who was a champion in America but an utter failure at stud in America and the United Kingdom, Bien Bien, and bargain for a reduced stud fee of three thousand pounds. Bien Bien was briefly brilliant in his racing career and is a handsome chestnut, but an examination of his pedigree when put together with Rewbell's yields nothing of promise. Bien Bien's pedigree is full of stamina influences, while Rewbell's is full of, well, nothing. Her fourth dam is unknown. Few recognizable Thoroughbred names inhabit her pedigree. But in 2000, she is set to visit the court of Bien Bien (that is, to be bred to him), and she gets in foal. On March 23, 2001, she foals a beautiful chestnut colt with a wide blaze face and four socks who will become the syndicate's darling, eventually named Dream Alliance. The real Rewbell is listed in the cast as playing herself, although a horse named Scarlett appears as Rewbell in her younger incarnation. Two younger horses—a foal named Buster and another young horse named Suzie—play Dream Alliance as he grows up. But Dream Alliance does indeed play himself as an adult, and he is an awesome horse and awesome actor.

Rewbell and her foal live on an "allotment," an empty lot strewn with garbage and unreliably fenced with chicken wire. Members of the syndicate bring all their table scraps and peelings to the allotment and throw them over the fence for the mare to eat, and the foal grows into a gorgeous colt who becomes the incarnation of all of the village's hopes and dreams. Janet Vokes says he is like a puppy, as he's so doted on by everyone. She talks to him; makes pacts with him that if he doesn't want to race, he'll always have a home with them; and thinks of him not as a horse but as a member of her family. For the first two years, the good people of Cefn Fforest deposit their ten pounds a week as Dream Alliance grows into a big, glorious horse, at which point Mr. and Mrs. Vokes visit the yard (training center) of well-known trainer Philip Hobbs. They are amazed at how posh it is, "like Shangri-La," and decide to send Dream to him. His snobby assistant trainer doesn't have much hope, but they agree to take him on. This street urchin of a horse doesn't have much speed, but he has the tenacity of a street fighter and heart to spare. He finishes fourth, second, and third in his first three races, attended by all members of the syndicate, and he wins his fourth, a steeplechase. The townsfolk are all deeply moved by the horse's accomplishments, and Howard, the accountant, says, "He doesn't ask for anything, and he gives you everything." They are all in love with their Dream, who keeps on winning.

Next, he finishes second to the great racehorse Denman in the Hennessy Gold Cup, while the syndicate members bring sandwiches and lager so they don't have to spend a lot on food at the races. These working class folk hobnob with elite society members, groomed and dressed beautifully, who watch their horses with cool aplomb while the syndicate jumps up and down and screams when Dream races. The apex of their success comes when Dream wins the Coral Welsh National Cup, the biggest race in Wales, and is sent to the Grand National, the biggest race in all of Britain.

Dream, however, is terribly injured in the race. His back hoof slices through a tendon in one of his forelegs, and vets want to put him down, as this is considered an irreparable injury. The only hope is a new treatment, stem cell therapy, which is also terribly expensive—it will cost about £20,000 and isn't guaranteed to work. The syndicate votes and unanimously agrees to spend the money to try to save their beloved horse. After sixteen months on the sidelines, Dream returns triumphant to the races.

Having owned a horse with an injured tendon who had stem cell therapy and returned to the races, I know that all the horse facts in *Dark Horse* are verifiable and true. That Dream's career is stopped when he is eight years old because he has begun to bleed in his lungs is also accurate for many racehorses. His tenacity is destroyed by the feeling that he is drowning in his own blood, unable to breathe, a common symptom in horses who run their hearts out. In this country, a drug called Salix (originally Lasix) is administered for this, though its use is much debated, and increasing numbers of tracks in the United States are against the use of the drug.

The heart of this film is Dream Alliance, his restoration of hope to a dying village, and the blow against the British caste system that still exists today, with lower classes separated from upper classes by a vast social gulf. The people of Cefn Fforest break the boundaries, and the town's syndicate becomes a national news story. But, really, this is a film about how profound human love for a horse can be. And Dream Alliance is as devoted to his people as his people are to him. As someone who isn't sentimental and doesn't like a feel-good film that plays on cheap and tawdry emotions, I found this documentary to be the real deal, as is Dream Alliance. This may be the most deeply felt, best horse film of all. Ultimately, each syndicate member wound up with a £1,400 disbursement at Dream's retirement. Shoppers in the local supermarket stopped and applauded Janet Vokes as she pushed her cleaning cart through the aisles. The rewards the syndicate received can't be measured in currency or trophies. What price can be put on the salvation of a whole village's soul because of a chestnut horse?

Dream Horse (2020)

In 2020, *Dark Horse* gave birth to *Dream Horse*, one of those "based on a true story" movies that I generally have contempt for (along with sentimental and feel-good movies), but the story of Dream Alliance and Janet Vokes is completely irresistible. Directed by Welsh television director Euros Lyn (1971–), this fictionalized version of *Dark Horse* is every bit as satisfying as its original. Toni Colette stars as Jan Vokes and Damian Lewis as Howard, the accountant, in a rare role in which he gets to demonstrate good humor, at odds with his rampant capitalist character in *Billions* (2016–) and his PTSD-damaged prisoner of war role in *Homeland* (2011–2020). My only minor critique is to wonder why the filmmakers felt the need to kill poor Rewbell at foaling—as if the film needed more tragedy than the utterly depressed village and people—presenting the Vokeses and other syndicate members with the burden of raising an orphan foal. Having raised orphan foals myself, I know that this is an exercise in exhaustion, as new babies must have their bottle of specially mixed horse formula every two to three hours. But for the Vokeses, it is a breeze, and Dream flourishes while the Vokeses display no dark circles under their eyes. Dream grows up a complete pet, loved by his people and loving them; Jan immediately treats him as a human—talking to him, making deals with him, giving him affection—and the horse, from infancy, responds with endless vocalizing and horse hugs. His emotion is revealed by magnificent close-ups of his soft, intelligent eyes. The film follows the trajectory of the documentary, although the fictional Dream Alliance doesn't run in the Grand National and injures himself instead in a stakes race; he is still rehabilitated with stem cell therapy and returns to triumph in the Welsh Grand National—this is very much a film about Welsh pride.

Euros Lyn cobbled together an excellent group of horsemen, enlisting graduates of *Game of Thrones* (2011–2019) and Ridley Scott's *Robin Hood* (2010) to ensure that Dream's races looked as real as possible and that Dream was as human as possible. Horse masters Daniel Naprous and Camille Naprous of The Devil's Horsemen, Peter White, and Tom Cox (also a stunt rider in *War Horse*) had all worked together previously, and the Cox family was also represented by stunt riders Jake and Chris Cox, with assists from Rebecca Horan, also from *Game of Thrones*, as assistant horse master. The production also utilized a lighter, smaller version of the revolutionary Steadicam, called a Stabileye, which was put into use first in 2017; the Stabileye was held by riders Chris Cox and Daniel Naprous to put the viewer right into the races in the most realistic race scenes in memory. Anyone who's seen footage from jockey cams mounted on riders' helmets can't imagine how much more thrilling the Stabileye system scenes can be. This results in even more "intimacy" with the almost human Dream Alliance. If you've seen *Dark Horse* and loved it, don't hesitate to see *Dream Horse*, which, unlike most "based on a true story" movies, manages to capture the great good feelings and honest emotion of the documentary (even featuring the real people, singing with the cast, behind the end titles).

5

Girls and Their Horses

The connection between girls and their horses is a mysterious one. OK, maybe not. It might be all about sex, having that great, sweating, fleet beast between your legs. But I digress. Some of the most beloved horses in all of film are owned by little girls—many of the girls orphans who have been badly injured in an accident and need the love of a horse to return them to the human race, who get help from curmudgeonly former jockeys or trainers who are likewise returned to sympathetic humanity by experiencing the love between girl and horse. At this point the horse is stolen or sold by an unsympathetic guardian or parent, breaking the girl's heart, or the horse is injured and uncaring adults want to euthanize it, but the girl insists she can nurse it back to health—melodrama and sentimentality abound.

National Velvet (1944) and *Giant* (1956)

The emblematic, original myth of girls and horses in the movies must certainly be *National Velvet* (1944), directed by the erstwhile Hollywood professional Clarence Brown (1890–1987), known for his talents working with impossible Greta Garbo and temperamental Joan Crawford, not easy customers for any director. So his success with twelve-year-old Elizabeth Taylor (1932–2011), nearly untried as a dramatic actress and equestrian, comes as no surprise. Brown wrangled difficult actresses, child actors, and horses with aplomb, and in *National Velvet*, he created a touchstone for the legions of girls who fell in love with horses, their majesty, elegance, beauty, and willing devotion, both in movies and in real life.

All we horse girls can identify with Velvet Brown and her instantaneous love of The Pie, a magnificent, spirited chestnut Thoroughbred gelding with a blaze and four socks, for whom fences are nothing more than a small obstacle. The Pie was born to jump, and Velvet was born to ride him. The Pie's real name was King Charles, and Elizabeth Taylor, who had been riding, supposedly, since she was three, first met and rode him in 1941, at Rancho Sea Air in Malibu, California. Just as Taylor's clichéd pushy stage mother campaigned for her beautiful daughter to get the part of Velvet, Taylor campaigned for King Charles to get his role. Egon Merz, who owned Rancho Sea Air, oversaw the training of King Charles and Elizabeth Taylor for the movie because, though the studio publicity machine published reams of praise for Taylor's equestrian abilities, she actually needed months of her own training and, eventually, a stunt double for the complex and dangerous scenes of racing at the Grand National Steeplechase.

The publicity machine had its own myth about King Charles: that he was a grandson of perhaps the greatest Thoroughbred racehorse and stallion of all time, Man o' War; however, no grandson of Man o' War named King Charles exists in the Jockey Club records, nor is there a birthday for any horse named King Charles that matches up with the *National Velvet* star's age. In truth, he was a seven-year-old Thoroughbred in 1944, purchased for $8,000 for the movie because, though naughty with most humans, he loved Elizabeth Taylor and could jump a car with ease. Plus, he was handsome, seemingly with the self-image of a matinee idol and with many a matinee idol's raffish personality: he was more than willing to bite and menace other crew and cast members despite being a teddy bear with Taylor. He was given to Taylor as a thirteenth birthday present

National Velvet, 1944. Elizabeth Taylor loves her Pie. Directed by Clarence Brown. (MGM/Photofest. ©MGM.)

after filming ended, and she kept him for the rest of his life. He died at twenty-four, after having lived the rest of his days at Rancho Sea Air in Malibu and still very much the darling of Taylor, though her stardom kept her from visiting often when she was working.

In the film, which is based on the 1935 novel of the same name, Velvet first sees The Pie running rampant in a field with his tail up in pure enjoyment; she and Mi (Mickey Rooney) watch from the road on their old cart with their old cart horse, a nag. They stop to watch him run, fearing he will run right through the fence of his paddock. Instead, he easily jumps the fence and runs off on the road to town, and Velvet is smitten—love at first sight. The Pie's owner despairs at the horse's continued naughty behavior and wants to be rid of him, so a town-wide lottery scheme is devised. Mi, an ex-jockey with a mysterious past, buys lottery tickets for all the Brown children. Of course, Velvet wins, and she becomes The Pie's owner. Also of course, The Pie allows her to ride him, though he disdains all other humans, and when she takes him over jumps and he magnificently clears them just as he did in his paddock, she and Mi hatch a scheme to take him to the most important steeplechase rase in England, the Grand National.

The Pie, in the course of his training, falls mysteriously ill, allowing Mi to demonstrate his hidden horse skills by treating the supine, moaning Pie with whiskey and hot water, though this happens off-screen so we have no idea how this medicinal course is given; focus is instead on Velvet's hysteria that she might lose The Pie to illness. This illness, however, bears no resemblance to any known horse ailment I ever encountered. Those who have written about the film assume the illness to be colic, an intestinal illness common in horses in general and Thoroughbreds in particular because of their high-strung personalities and high-protein diets, supposedly; anyone who works with horses knows that you can cause a colic by looking at a horse cross-eyed. However, I have, unfortunately, witnessed and treated many horses with colic (we have today an excellent drug called Banamine that can be injected, despite the wonders of whiskey and hot water), and I have never seen one like this. Typically, a colicking horse will display great discomfort, stretching and rolling in an attempt to ease the pain in its gut. Sometimes an actual torsion of the intestine will be the cause, and expensive surgery might be necessary. The age-old treatment for colic is endless walking of the horse, trying to get the intestine to untwist or the gas to release (horses are prone to this because they are unable to vomit). If walking doesn't work, forcing the horse to run in a paddock or a round pen might. I cured a colicky horse this way once when a colt of mine became ill late on a Saturday night; he was rolling in pain with his ears pinned and his eyes full of tears, and I knew that getting him to a hospital that late would take forever. But The Pie just lies flat and, after a terrible night of waiting and worrying for Velvet, gets up the next morning, seemingly cured. Anyone who knows horses realizes that this mystery illness is pure fiction, created for moviegoers instead of horse caretakers. In terms of points of inaccuracy, there is one detail the movie changed to get right, at least. In the book, The Pie is named aptly because he is a piebald, or spotted, horse; however, no Thoroughbreds are spotted, and non-Thoroughbreds are not allowed in the Grand National Stee-plechase. So the now appropriately colored Pie loses his spots but keeps his name.

Regardless of the true-to-life details of the illness, The Pie survives and is able to go on to the Grand National. After a jockey mix-up, Velvet, dressed in jockey's silks and pants and having cut her hair so she would resemble a boy, rides The Pie in the Grand National and wins, as many other competitors fall and crumple at various difficult, dangerous jumps. She is only revealed as a girl (women were not allowed to pilot horses at that time, especially in the Grand National) when she faints just after the finish line from the exertion and emotion and the track doctor unbuttons her silks to listen to her heart. Though the victory is taken from her, she becomes a heroine to the nation, and The Pie becomes a famous horse hero. For horse girls, there is also the incipient thrill of early feminism: a woman can compete with men when it comes to riding ability and can win at the highest level. What horse girl hasn't dreamed that dream? I have a memory from when I was quite young of driving home with my father from a day at the races at now defunct Hollywood Park, and on the freeway, a truck towing a horse trailer full of beautiful racehorses pulled by us as I watched in wonderment at the reality that some people own and transport horses through the world.

Elizabeth Taylor continues as the original horse girl for the ages in the epic though dated 1956 film *Giant*. It transpires over the course of three long hours, but only the first hour is worth watching and only for the great horse, War Winds, and the performance of James Dean, who died before the movie was released. Dean seems to be acting in a different movie from everyone else—he inhabits his character, Jett Rink, with the drawl, the cowboy slouch, the irreverence. Elizabeth Taylor and Rock Hudson are old-fashioned actors, clearly acting, but Dean does something entirely different. In the last two hours, everyone becomes falsely old, with blue-gray highlights in their hair and drawn-on crows' feet, and even Dean looks silly as old Jett Rink. The film features a racist, misogynistic main character, Jordan (Rock Hudson), who finally becomes aware that Mexicans are people and women have ideas. It is a most unapologetic, damning portrayal of Texas (where I lived and had a horse ranch for five years and found the Texas of the 1950s and the Texas of the 1990s to be remarkably the same). In a way, the film must be commended for its undercurrent of recognition of racism and misogyny and its attempt to deal with both realistically.

A horse named War Winds, played by Highland Dale (1943–1973), the star stallion of owner/trainer/breeder of champion working Quarter Horses Ralph McCutcheon, motivates the plot of *Giant* early on. A Texas gazillionaire and land and cattle baron named Jordan Benedict (Rock Hudson) has come east to Maryland to look at and purchase a horse to improve his broodmares' bloodlines. From his private train car, he first sees Leslie (Elizabeth Taylor) foxhunting on War Winds, and when the two of them ride up to him at the

Lytton Farm, Benedict falls for both instantly. Benedict returns to Texas with both a new bride, Leslie, and a new horse.

But problems arise as soon as they arrive in the Lone Star state. Benedict's unmarried, tough older sister, Luz (Mercedes McCambridge), rules the ranch with an iron hand and clearly has psychosexual issues: she tries to situate Benedict and Leslie in separate bedrooms, resents Leslie's presence, and condescends to her in a strange, incestuous rivalry.

Rounding up cattle, with Leslie being taken back to the house because of the relentless Texas heat, Luz decides to ride War Winds, even though no one but Leslie is supposed to be allowed on him. Taking her dislike of Leslie out on the horse, Luz spurs the frightened, angry horse over and over in a series of shots much admired by Martin Scorsese, who notes the brilliance of cutting from a wide shot of War Winds trying to buck Luz off to intense close-ups of her spurs being dug into the horse's side. Soon thereafter, we see the forlorn, limping horse, riderless, returning to the Benedict home as if looking for his beloved Leslie, while in the house, Luz, unconscious from hitting her head when unseated, is tended by a doctor. War Winds did indeed buck her off; she hit her head on a mesquite stump and almost immediately died. Ranch hands are seen tending to the horse. In the best scene of the film (for horse lovers), Leslie goes to the injured horse, horrified, and then runs into the house to find out what has transpired. The look of longing and sadness that War Winds gives as she rushes off is heartrending. "Why have you brought me to this land of barbarians?" he seems to be saying with his big, tragic eyes. Indeed, Leslie finds Texas barbaric and backward too, so that she and the horse are metaphorically twinned, though Leslie fights to keep her spirit and beliefs.

My only complaint with the first hour has to do with the failure to call a veterinarian for such an expensive, well-bred horse: surely such a huge outfit would have a resident veterinarian for the 500,000 cattle and hundreds of horses on the place. But no vet appears, no X-rays are taken, and Benedict tells Leslie that he had to shoot the horse because its leg was broken. When I lived in Texas, all of the big horse and cattle ranches had resident veterinarians, as both horses and cows are accidents or suicides waiting to happen, and expensive stallions like War Winds had vet attention if they coughed once or limped slightly. So this aspect of the film strains credibility.

My other issue is that when spirited, emotional Leslie is told that Benedict has shot her horse, she exhibits a stunning lack of anger or grief. This is inexplicable, as we were led to believe she loves War Winds. The need to move the plot on overwhelms what should have been a great acting moment for Elizabeth Taylor, and any horse lover who has lost a beloved horse knows the pain of such a loss.

Highland Dale, who played War Winds, was a star in his own right, having won numerous PATSY Awards (Performing Animal Top Star of the Year—the Oscars and Emmys combined of the animal world) under various names, usually the name of the horse in the TV show or movie—it's been noted that his trainer originally called him Beauty or Beaut when he discovered Dale as an eighteen-month-old colt. The PATSY was first awarded in 1951, to Francis the Talking Mule, and was begun by the American Humane Society. The awards evolved to include different categories of animals—dogs, cats, horses, and wild animals—and were popular and even televised, much like the Oscars and Emmys are. Such luminaries as Trigger, Lassie, Rin Tin Tin, and Silver won PATSYs. Hosted by such celebrities as Betty White, Allen Ludden, and Bob Barker, the PATSYs disappeared when their funding dried up in 1986. And that was the end of the PATSYs.

Highland Dale became the second-highest-earning animal performer, having made $500,000 for owner/trainer Ralph McCutcheon; he was second only to Lassie (though the Lassie issue surely is in question, as numerous dogs played Lassie over the years). Highland Dale was an American Saddlebred horse (a gaited, elegant breed dating back to the Revolutionary War) with a recognizable head, free of the dish-faced Arabian influence and quite masculine. Black with a small white star, Highland Dale was best known as the eponymous attraction in the television show *Fury*, beginning in 1955, for which he earned $1,500 an episode, more than star Peter Graves. He also appeared in episodes of the TV series *Bonanza*, *The High Chaparral*, *Lassie*, and *The Adventures of Rin Tin Tin*, giving him a virtual monopoly in television, not to mention his starring roles in movies, including the 1946 film version of *Black Beauty*, *Outlaw Stallion*, *Gypsy Colt*, *Wild Is the Wind*, and many others. The makers of *Giant* felt lucky to get his star power for the cameo turn as War Winds. The tragic sentience the horse demonstrates rivals James Dean's scrupulous method and realism.

Little Miss Marker (1934)

Little Miss Marker (1934) is a horse of a different color, neither fully a girl-and-horse tale nor a racetrack tale; it is a pre-Code film based on a Damon Runyon story, with typical Damon Runyonesque–stylized dialogue, featuring contractionless sentences littered with gangster-ese and typical Runyonesque nicknames. It opens with a gang of thugs planning to throw a horse race. Big Steve's (Charles Bickford) horse Dream Prince has won a few races in a row, thanks to a crooked vet's "speed ball" concoction, and will be the favorite in the next race. Big Steve and his vet plan to let the horse race drug free so that he will certainly lose while putting out gossip that Dream Prince has never been better and will surely win. But the plan is much more odious. Supposedly, the horse's heart can only take one more speed ball—another drugged race will surely get him a win and also surely kill him. So allowing Dream Prince to lose the impending race will ensure much better odds on him in the next race, and Big Steve is more than willing to kill the horse for those great odds. This is all fine with the bookie Sorrowful Jones (Adolphe Menjou), who will gladly conspire and take the action as he will surely profit from being in on the scam. No one seems troubled by the plan to kill the horse.

Indeed, as the narrative progresses, the betting action is fast and furious at Sorrowful Jones's office; one man arrives to place his bet with a way too adorable daughter in tow: six-year-old Shirley Temple. The man, however, has no money and wants Sorrowful to take his "marker"—that is, let him owe Jones the twenty dollars, which he promises to pay. Jones, known as the biggest tightwad in the business (much attention is paid to his worn suit: he is too cheap to buy new clothes), hesitates. So the clearly desperate man declares he will leave his daughter as collateral, and for reasons unknown, Jones agrees.

The man never returns for his daughter, and later, we learn that he committed suicide when Dream Prince lost. The child, now called "Marky" because she was left as a marker, is cared for by Sorrowful Jones and Big Steve's "kept" girlfriend, Bangles (Dorothy Dell), and in no time at all, she is talking gangster-ese, calling losing horses "bang tail nags," and saying of herself, "I ain't no sissy." She also gives the gangsters nicknames after the Knights of the Round Table because her mother, before she died, used to read Marky bedtime stories of King Arthur and his court. She meets Dream Prince when he is about to be shipped to his race and declares him "her charger," as he is a handsome, calm, friendly sort, except when Big Steve gets close to him. Dream Prince is terrified of Big Steve; when the man approaches him, he rears with terror in his widened eyes, their whites showing, and vocalizes his fear with a shrieking whinny. The horse realizes Steve's murderous intent.

Many hijinks ensue, including the important information that Sorrowful has long been crazy about Bangles, and after Bangles spends the night at Sorrowful's apartment because she falls asleep while singing to Marky, it appears that Bangles has been intimate with Sorrowful while Big Steve is out of town. Bangles's posh apartment comes with a maid who is on Big Steve's payroll, so of course this apparent tryst is reported to Big Steve.

The set piece of the whole film is Bangles's attempt to return Marky to her former delightful innocence, by closing down Big Steve's nightclub and having all the gangsters dress up as medieval knights. The party includes Dream Prince, who is brought to the event and dressed in a medieval horse's garb. Marky is put on his back while all the knights parade around the nightclub, singing wise guy songs in celebration. Marky, delighted, resumes her belief in "fairy" stories (just as she has been taught by a reluctant Jones how to pray, and when she does, she asks God to get Jones a new suit of clothes, which touches him).

Then, chaos strikes. Big Steve returns from Chicago, armed, and barges into his club and accuses Bangles of consorting with Jones during his absence. Aghast that his horse has been included in this medieval re-creation, he approaches Dream Prince, whose eyes widen with terror once more (this horse could really act!), and the horse rears, throwing Marky to the floor and knocking her unconscious. The horse's sentience, revealed by his fear of the man who injects him with speed balls, becomes the device that moves the plot forward.

Marky's injury is severe enough that she requires a blood transfusion to survive; suffice it to say that Big Steve's blood is the only match among the gangsters for Marky's. He is told that he has good, strong blood by the doctors and nurses, and it is as if this is the first time Big Steve has ever been told he's good for something; he is transformed. He leaves, allowing Jones and Bangles to live, and thanks to the horse's fear of Steve and all that has transpired, Bangles and Jones will get together and raise Marky as their own. *Little Miss Marker* turns out to be a girl-and-her-horse movie as full of sentiment as any other, if it does at first masquerade as a gangster yarn and as a Knights of the Round Table farce, with its strangely stilted and funny dialogue.

The phenomenon of this film is Shirley Temple, who was born in 1928 and therefore only five or six when this film was made. The child is a prodigy. She hasn't yet turned into the too-cute older version of herself and is genuinely adorable; she recites her lines believably and learns songs with Bangles. I've never enjoyed Shirley Temple movies because of her over-the-top cuteness. However, in *Little Miss Marker*, only her second feature, Shirley Temple was preciousness and perfection exemplified, and she is still a real child; even I was won over.

Supposedly, in one scene with Bangles, in which Bangles disapproves of the child's new lingo, numerous takes were required because Dell couldn't stop her own laughter when hearing this tiny girl speaking like a gangster. Dell is the other marvel of the film, like a young Mae West, playing the classic bad girl with a heart of gold (Jones always calls Bangles Golddigger), but unfortunately shortly after this film was completed, Dell died at the age of nineteen in a drunken car wreck after a night of partying. The film was remade several times, but the charm of Temple and Dell could never be re-created.

My Friend Flicka (1943)

Honorable mention must be made for *My Friend Flicka* (1943), which boasts Rex the Devil Horse's trainer, Jack Lindell, and the one and only Monty Roberts, the self-declared horse whisperer, in charge of stunts filmed in Utah: a blue-blooded pedigree for any horse film. In fact, Lindell pulls out his old Rex trick for Flicka: getting the star horse tangled up in rope or barbed wire. And furthermore, he creates a title filly who is as sentient as Rex: she makes eye contact, verbalizes, vocalizes, and is very much both a character in the film and a mover of narrative. The family farm pretending to be a real horse farm is full of barbed-wire fences and pole corrals, a sorry way to keep horses.

But the real heart of the film—directed by Harold Schuster (1902–1986), who is known as being the director of the first three-strip Technicolor film produced in England, *Wings of the Morning* (1937)—is the young Roddy McDowall as Ken, a dreamy, sensitive youth, who was fifteen at the time of filming but looks far younger because he is such a small boy and who speaks with a slight British accent (a mystery, as he is supposed to be an American farm boy). What is striking, aside from his acting, is McDowall's clear connection with the filly who plays Flicka and his utter lack of fear around the horses. He's adorable, and his love for horses and his need to have a horse of his own make him as obsessive and vulnerable as any horse girl. Plus, he can really ride.

Flicka, named by the Swedish American farmhand Gus, is supposedly Swedish for "little girl." She is the yearling daughter of a valuable mare on the farm, but her father was the crazy stallion Albino, about whom Ken's father gripes endlessly. The alpha stud on the farm is Banner, whose intelligence deters a stampede over cliffs by the herd. It isn't clear what breed of horse this family raises, though an idiotic subplot has a neighbor who races horses buying Flicka's mother for racing. A broodmare turned into a race horse? Unlikely, and utterly unrealistic, but this will help save the struggling family farm. Unfortunately, the crazy mare, loaded onto the back of a truck to go to the neighbor's farm, rears and strikes her head at the ranch's entrance, falling instantly dead.

Every horse girl trope is called up to put Flicka in peril within the movie, from the mountain lion she saves Ken's father from to her seemingly about-to-be fatal illness, with Ken's parents desiring to euthanize her to ease her suffering. But Ken's parents have hearts after all; they can't do it, especially after the rescue from the mountain lion.

The best scene, though probably not the most realistic, is when Ken halterbreaks Flicka at his dad's behest. The filly has come to love and trust Ken, and of course, he adores her and spends all his time with her. So when his father tells him to take off his belt and loop it around Flicka's neck, she accepts this strangeness with complete belief in Ken's love for her. Then his father says he should take his kerchief out of his pocket, and loop it through the belt, to use as a lead. Ken does so, and Flicka is immediately receptive and willing as Ken leads her around her small pen with kerchief and belt. Ken glows with pride and delight. His father hands him a halter with a lead already attached to it and tells Ken to put it on her. Ken balks at first, not sure how to accomplish this, but the filly stands still and gentle as Ken puts the halter on her and removes his belt from her neck, leading her again around the pen. This scene cements and illuminates the bond between Ken and Flicka; however, as someone who has halterbroken many a difficult weanling and yearling, I can attest to the ruckus that usually ensues. A yearling who has never worn a halter or been led will not go willingly. I always would put halters on my foals as soon as they were ready to go outside and usually attached a part of a dog leash to the halter, so if the baby needed grabbing, it was easy, though still likely to be a battle. My babies were spoiled rotten, like Flicka, and given all the adoration and attention that Flicka gets, but haltering and leading were always tense and dangerous. If only all fillies were like Flicka!

Another issue in *My Friend Flicka*, and one also found in *National Velvet* and *Giant*, is the total absence of vets. When Flicka becomes sick nearly unto death, no veterinarian is called. She relies on lame-brained home remedies and love to continue to live. Was the ability to call a vet born in the second half of the twentieth century? In both *Giant* and *My Friend Flicka*, euthanasia was enacted with rifle or pistol to the head. I'm glad I had horses in the era in which veterinarians had been invented.

My Friend Flicka had a sequel, *Thunderhead, Son of Flicka* (1945), and gave birth to numerous remakes and television series, so clearly it pushed the right buttons in the heads of horse lovers. The shame was that Roddy McDowall was assigned to character roles as he aged (even playing a chimp in *Planet of the Apes*) instead of currying his sensitive talent as a leading man.

The Horse Whisperer (1998)

But even those of us who are cynical about all things human may shed a tear at a girl-and-horse film because we recognize this special bond. The brilliance of *The Horse Whisperer* (1998), which manages to bring together nearly all of the possible melodramatic tropes: the hurt girl (she actually loses part of one leg!), the hurt horse that the woman vet wants to euthanize right after the ghastly accident (one might believe a macho vet might euthanize too soon, but a wide-faced, wide-eyed Cherry Jones playing the woman vet? The case must indeed be serious), the citified, sort of British parents who simply don't get it, the monosyllabic horse trainer whose heart has once been broken by a city woman much like the girl's effete mother (embodied by Robert Redford—if he whispered in my ear, I'd listen too,). And the girl is played by the young, beautiful Scarlett Johansson, in the tradition of Elizabeth Taylor and *National Velvet*, because gorgeous young girls love their horses even more than plain girls can imagine. In fact, *The Horse Whisperer* will also appear in these pages again, as it is a unique collection of horse plots and themes designed to pluck at our heartstrings and teach us useful elements of horse training, such as horses' dislike of cell phones. The horse, Pilgrim, steals the show, as he is magnificent at first and then so badly maimed as to be unrecognizable, both physically and emotionally. Both he and the girl are returned to the world of the living from their twilight zones, thanks to patience, training, and love. And the mere presence of the handsome horse whisperer, Robert Redford, makes the film a standout. Redford is that unique thing in Hollywood, the real deal: he actually owns horses, knows horses, and rides horses, so directing and starring in this film seemed a natural fit for him. He isn't "playing" a horseman; he *is* a horseman.

The Black Stallion (1979)

In another anomaly like *My Friend Flicka*, substitute a boy for Velvet of *National Velvet* and a shipwreck for the stultifying small-town life that Velvet endures until the magical moment when she falls in love with The Pie, and you've got *The Black Stallion* (1979), a film in which the horse's sentience and ability to communicate both with humans and other horses is a given. I dare any horse lover not to adore this film. It's no coincidence that the eponymous black stallion is called The Black, just as in *National Velvet* the horse is called The Pie—coloration is destiny in horse movies. The Black, as an Arabian stallion, officially couldn't compete against Thoroughbreds in normal Thoroughbred horse races, but he becomes the third entry in a much-touted match race between the champion Thoroughbred from the West Coast against the champion Thoroughbred from the East Coast, reminiscent of the near-mythic match race on November 1, 1938, between horse-of-the-common-man Seabiscuit and bred-to-the-purple War Admiral (Seabiscuit won handily). Arabians are far slower than Thoroughbreds; what they do have is endurance. The match race is set at two miles, a very unusual length for a Thoroughbred race, the longest of which, in reality, are a mile and a half (the Belmont Stakes, for example, the third leg of the Triple Crown). This race, which The Black wins easily after a terrible start and a bleeding leg injury, therefore doesn't strain credibility, as the two-mile distance, while very long for a Thoroughbred, is well within the wheelhouse of a talented Arabian.

The boy in the movie, Alexander Ramsay (played by the remarkable Kelly Reno), first sees the black stallion while he is on shipboard with his father. The horse, being handled by a bevy of cruel, terrified Arabs, goes wild, rearing and snorting and whinnying, trying to strike his handlers with his front hooves; he is refusing to enter a cabin turned into a stall for him and knows nothing of submission to humans. The boy, wide-eyed at this display of anger and will, returns to the horse's stall with sugar cubes, which he sets on the porthole of the stall and which the horse munches with dispatch. I have to add here that I have never known a horse to eat sugar cubes. Carrots and peppermints, yes, and a stalled horse once stole my uneaten sandwich, but sugar cubes? To me, this would seem to be a bit of mythology begun in western movies.

That night, the ship mysteriously wrecks, catches fire, explodes, and sinks, but before this can happen, courageous Alex runs to the horse's stall, cuts his bonds, and opens his cabin door, saving him from certain drowning. Alex and the horse seem to be the only survivors of this tragedy, and the horse, swimming for all he's worth, his cut ropes trailing behind him, is the vehicle of Alex's salvation, as Alex is able to swim to the horse and tie one of the ropes around his waist. Though knocked unconscious by the explosion, the boy is taken to shore by the horse.

What follows is a full half an hour of no dialogue, as the boy is stranded on the deserted island (in reality, Sardinia) alone with the wild horse. The beauty of this portion of the movie is unequaled in horse films, as the horse, the Arabian Champion Cass Ole (1969–1993), runs, wide-striding, against the ocean and the setting sun. Much like King Kong on Skull Island, The Black's mastery over all in this new world is not questionable. But first the boy must repay the favor the horse did him: he finds the horse, snagged by his multiple ropes and tack, on some jagged rocks. He fights mightily, vocalizing the whole time with angry snorts and pitiful whinnying. The boy cuts him loose, at great peril because of the thrashing hooves and the heaving horse. The wildness and passion of this horse move Alex deeply. Shortly thereafter, the boy, asleep on the beach, is menaced by a horrifying hissing, spitting, tongue-flicking cobra, but the horse once again comes to the rescue, battering the snake to death with his hooves.

Alex collects some seaweed in a huge seashell and approaches the horse, who comes to him to eat. The boy then offers seaweed from his hand, and after a dance of approach and retreat, the horse takes this too, cementing a camaraderie that results in boy and horse playing tag, chasing each other, and frolicking on the beach and even into the water so that Alex is able to swim to the horse and mount him. Rapturous, boy and horse gallop on the beach in newfound friendship. It should be noted that the director, Carroll Ballard, was also a cinematographer with a renowned eye for beauty; his cinematographer for this project, Caleb Deschanel, is equally known for the beauty of his work. These two make this dialogue-free romp into an unforgettable miracle of oneness: the boy and horse have a tangible connection in perfect happiness and rapport.

One hates to leave the wordless island, but Italian sailors chance upon it and retrieve the boy and the horse. Once home, The Black lives in a suburban backyard in late 1940s America, and the boy sleeps on the ground near him, eschewing bedroom and bed, to the dismay of his mother (Teri Garr). Through a series of misadventures, The Black and the boy find their way to Henry (Mickey Rooney), a once-renowned horse trainer, and The Black becomes the mystery horse in the big match race, ridden, of course, by the boy, who equals Velvet for courage and grit.

The Black Stallion is matchless for equine vocalizing. Valerie Koutnik O'Conor, the equine sounds consultant, creates a veritable language for the horse. Both The Black and the white carriage horse, Napoleon, owned by Henry's friend, converse with humans as well. The Black seems utterly wild on the island and pretty cantankerous stateside, thanks to the magnificent training job of Corky Randall (1929–2009), who achieved the endless horse action with visual cues to all the horses, such as raising and shaking a whip. Randall cited Cass Ole as his favorite actor, saying, "He was so smart and such a character. He was almost human." As well, Cass Ole had five doubles for swimming, racing, and running free; specifically, for the swimming scenes, two white French Carmargue horses were used, and they had to be painted black. Cass Ole himself had a blaze face and socks, so he, too, had to be made up to play The Black.

The boy, however, was the real thing. Kelly Reno was found through newspaper ads seeking a youth who could really ride, and he was perfection. Born in 1966, he was raised on a cattle ranch in Colorado and had been riding since he was three. Though doubles were used for some of the more dangerous scenes, Reno did the majority of the riding in the film, frequently bareback and with no hands, his arms raised in the air in ecstasy. This was clearly a boy who loved horses, and this horse in particular. Reno was also a sincere and affectless actor, and he hoped for a career in films after graduating from college. However, a serious car crash, in which his car was hit by a semitrailer, resulted in critical injuries and a lengthy period of recuperation. He would never act again, aside from *The Black Stallion* and its two sequels. Unlike the horse, which could not be tamed or civilized, Reno's fate was far worse.

Aside from the anomaly of an Arabian running against Thoroughbreds, only one scene stands out as impossible. Henry arranges to work the horse in the dark for the preeminent racing broadcaster of the time, to demonstrate the horse's speed and ability, in an attempt to get him into the match race. Knowing racetracks, I would assume this would be in the very early morning. A raging thunderstorm occurs, but this doesn't stop the work from happening. Horses are lightning magnets; every year in Kentucky, horses turned out in posh paddocks die from being struck, and on racetracks, racing is halted completely when thunderstorms occur because of the danger to horses and riders. Not in this movie. The work occurs in the crackling of the storm, and poor Alex returns, unconscious, another nod to fainting Velvet at the end of the Grand National. The boy has ridden courageously, just like Velvet, but any racetrack veteran like Henry would never risk horse and rider in such a storm. This makes for dramatic and beautiful cinema but is far from the truth. Nevertheless, the broadcaster ignites the wonderful story of the Mystery Horse, and The Black gets into the race.

The Black has opinions that he willingly communicates on every occasion and circumstance, and his eyes shine with sentience and emotion. In the scenes that require him to go wild, those intelligent eyes sparkle with fury. One fully understands the boy's utter enchantment with the horse: Who wouldn't adore him? Though this is called a "family film," in reality it is a horse lover's film, as anyone who has had a bond with a certain horse will comprehend and be empathetic to the love between the boy and The Black. This film depends on the notion of equine sentience to succeed, which it does brilliantly.

Dreamer (2005)

Mash up the same themes, and you've got *Dreamer* (2005), a film much loved in the Thoroughbred community but virtually unknown outside of it. It is the only directorial attempt of writer/actor John Gatins (1968–) and wasn't well-reviewed for its rote, sentimental approach to the material; it barely recouped its $32 million budget. In it, a promising Thoroughbred filly suffers what should be not only a career-ending but also a life-ending injury, and the owner wants to euthanize her. But the small daughter of a down-and-out trainer wants to try to save the filly, in whom she sees something special. Make that child Dakota Fanning, of the big eyes and gleaming smile, and her father (Kurt Russell) doesn't have a chance of saying no. There's the necessary scene of Cale (Fanning) put into grave danger when she tries to run away by riding Sonador off into the sunset, and things go awry, as they must, before the film reaches its heartwarming conclusion.

I'm no fan of "based on a true story" movies, because no true story fits into the watch works of the screenplay structure (though I am a stickler for true horse knowledge in horse films), but the filly, Sonador, in this film is based on a favorite real mare, Mariah's Storm. She lived through such an injury to race again and then foaled one of the best stallions in the world, the now-deceased Iron Horse, Giant's Causeway. He finished second by a short head in the Breeders' Cup Classic because his jockey dropped a rein—the intelligent horse flicked his ears back and forth, trying to comprehend the message the jockey was giving, when, in reality, the message was, "I'm an idiot for dropping the rein in the biggest race in the world." I fell madly in love with Giant's Causeway the first time I saw him, as he was utter equine perfection, and have had the privilege to breed mares to him twice. Mariah's Storm's legacy in Thoroughbred history is cemented because of her top-class son and her grandsons now standing at stud, so a movie based on her life and near death moves me deeply.

You've got to love Sonador. She eats popsicles, carries Cale's backpack, follows the girl around like a puppy, and returns a nightmare-addled ex-jockey to the saddle to give him the biggest win of any jockey's career, the Breeders' Cup Classic. She's got tons of personality. But the movie is so fraught with horse-related errors that if you know anything about horses and Kentucky, it will drive you nuts. As one minor example, Ben Crane (Kurt Russell) has "Crane Horse Farm" on his truck door. Many horse farms have trucks and SUVs driving around with logos and farm names on them, but not one includes the word *horse*: in Kentucky, that's a given. You see these vehicles all around Lexington that read "Three Chimneys" or "Lane's End," and it's assumed that you'll know they're horse farms. If you don't, to hell with you.

When Sonador breaks down in her race, the track vet who runs out to treat her instantly diagnoses a broken cannon bone, the large bone of the horse's shin. But how can he know? It's not a compound fracture, no bone sticking out of the skin. It's nondisplaced, we learn later. X-ray vision? Has *Dreamer* turned sci-fi on us?

And the hurry to put such an expensive stakes-winning filly down? Ridiculous. The owner, a rich Arab oil prince, would go to great lengths to save her for his broodmare band. But drama must be created, so everyone is in a hurry to make Sonador dead. And why would a rich prince have one horse with a down-and-out trainer like Ben Crane? In the real world of racing, the Maktoums, the family on whom the rich sheikh is based (the Maktoum family is the ruling family of Dubai and are heavily invested in racing, which is terrific for the sport), have prominent trainers working for them, with whom they have large strings of horses in training. One Sonador, with one Ben Crane, makes no sense.

And then there's the breeding nonsense—drives me crazy, since I have bred Thoroughbred racehorses for decades. Ben and Cale visit Ashford Stud—a place I have bred at innumerable times and where the aforementioned Giant's Causeway stood at stud—and look at Grand Slam, a wonderful stallion, certainly, but he never stood for $200,000. Ashford supposedly lowers the price to $15,000 for Ben "to cover their expenses," the non-Irish head of Ashford tells them. First of all, there are no non-Irishmen in positions of power at Ashford. Second, Ashford would jump at the chance to do a foal share with a mare of Sonador's quality. A foal share is when you put up the mare, Ashford (or any other farm) puts up the stallion season, and you share the proceeds from the foal, at no expense to you other than mare and foal care.

Ashford is an international operation, the largest owner of stallions in the world—they wouldn't have to "cover expenses" for a single breeding that would take fifteen minutes of their time. Finally, the Ashford guy tells Ben he can have a breeding slot in the first week of May—that's all that Grand Slam has open, as he's booked for the whole year. What rubbish! Stallions are booked day by day, and sometimes hour by hour and minute by minute, not well in advance, because a mare's heat cycle is impossible to predict. In fact, Ashford Stud's booking secretaries are among the most brilliant and helpful, always finding the spot you want, or close to it, when you call in with a ready mare, even if that spot is an added ten at night rendezvous. These scenes in no way represent the reality of breeding in Kentucky—they are a Hollywood fantasyland version, and they are more than irksome to knowledgeable viewers.

Then there's a particular bit of silliness in *Dreamer* that arises as necessary to return Sonador to the races. The vet comes out to Ben's farm to tell him he's done tests on Sonador (blood tests? DNA mapping?) that reveal she can never get pregnant. What hogwash! There are no "tests" for breeding soundness. In the real world, the reproductive vet inserts an ultrasound device to view the mare's vaginal canal and has a look at her ovaries and uterus to determine when and if the mare is ready to be bred. In decades of working with Thoroughbred broodmares, I have never had a vet tell me that a mare can never get pregnant—with modern veterinary medicine, there are fixes for nearly every reproductive issue as long as the mare has ovaries and a uterus, and in my experience, all of them do. If the vet had ultrasounded Sonador, he would have known on the spot if she didn't. He wouldn't have had to return from "tests" to tell Ben about Sonador's condition. But a vet with his rubber-gloved arm up a mare's backside isn't exactly cinema magic. A non-horsey visitor to my farm witnessed this phenomenon and, years later, said of it, "I still wake up screaming."

Further frustrating inaccuracies are found in the prerace shenanigans in *Dreamer*. In the saddling paddock (at beautiful Keeneland Racetrack in Lexington), the racing manager for the sheikh has his stallion brought over for a photo opportunity with Sonador, and much raring and pawing ensues. I have been to many races at Keeneland and other tracks, and watched countless more on television, and this would never happen. What idiot would endanger his animal right before the biggest race of the animal's life, with a multimillion-dollar purse and huge future stud fees at risk? After this run in with the stallion, Sonador looks fine, but Ben feels her now-healed leg and says, "I feel heat in it." Now come on—when there's heat in a leg, it's because an injury has caused it to become swollen. It doesn't happen instantly—Ben might feel heat in Sonador's leg the next morning, but not immediately.

And yet, I really like this movie and loved Sonador (who was played, by the way, by numerous horses with various abilities—including a mechanical one in some of the race scenes). Sonador's plight tugs at your heartstrings, and in the end, Luis Guzman, as Sonador's groom, gets to utter the true and emblematic line, "Girls and horses are the most magical thing."

Marnie (1964)

I've saved the strangest "girls and their horses" film for last: Alfred Hitchcock's (1899–1980) 1964 film, *Marnie*, a reviled flop when it was released but now beloved by film critics as a masterpiece. The title character, Marnie (Tippi Hedren), is high strung, fearful of stormy weather, and neurotic and runs away from difficult situation after difficult situation that she herself has created. Do those characteristics remind you of anything? Of course, Marnie is a Thoroughbred horse (as she herself says on the phone to her mother at one point, describing her bout with flu, "I'm still a little hoarse"); her thieving and kleptomania are powered by fear, just as fear powers some of the Thoroughbred's running prowess. She's an ace handicapper at the track: she understands horses on a level that is never fully explained in the film but that ultimately seems clear: she is, indeed, a little horse.

As such, she fascinates businessman Mark Rutledge (Sean Connery), whose hobby is zoology and taming predatory species. Early on he tells Marnie that he is proud of having tamed a jaguarundi. When Marnie asks him what he trained the animal to do, Mark answers, "Trust me." He sees Marnie as another wild thing he might be able to tame, a good challenge, as he also states he has an interest in predatory females. But Marnie is the typical blond, glacial Hitchcock female character, and not even Sean Connery—at that time thought to be the most irresistible man in the world, having played James Bond—lights her up. French film theorist Raymond Bellour suggests that Mark's attraction to Marnie is fetishistic, reducing Marnie to what she does: she is a compulsive thief. Certainly, taming wild things might suggest this. As well, Hitchcock's voyeuristic camera fetishizes Marnie throughout the film, from the opening shot in which the camera is lovingly focused on her backside as she walks through a train station.

What does light her up and makes her eyes go all soft and warm is her horse, Forio (the name of a picturesque Italian town on the island of Ischia). She talks to him (and he will eventually talk back), kisses him, and snuggles his muzzle with her face, and he is called her "old spoiled rotten baby." When Marnie rides him, they are one, and she is, for the moment, free; her tied up blond hair breaks loose and flies behind her head, flowing much like the horse's mane and tail. Forio is clearly her spirit animal, her freedom, and her love. The psychosexual attraction of women to horses must be considered a subtext here, since the film is so involved in psychobabble and phony Freudianism; men repel Marnie, but she adores Forio, her man replacement. Mark, an amateur analyst, thinks he can cure Marnie's screaming nightmares and inability to quit stealing money from wherever she works.

When Mark blackmails Marnie into marrying him (including a honeymoon rape scene out of Hitchcock's imagination—or perhaps not totally, for Hitchcock is rumored to have mistreated Hedren due to his unrequited affection), he brings Forio to the family estate at which he and Marnie live, as Mark's father is a horse fancier with a glamorous, too-tidy barn full of horses. When she sees her horse, again, her eyes go all soft and warm, she kisses him, and jumps on him bareback in her flowing chiffon nightgown, galloping off and jumping a fence, into the woods. Forio is Marnie's ultimate escape vehicle, her wild side.

In one pivotal scene, Marnie goes on a hunt with Mark's father and a dozen other people, complete with hunt outfits, elegant horses, and hounds. When the hounds fall on a feckless fox and tear it apart, Marnie is triggered by the blood (or generally the color red) into a full-fledged terror (along with lightning and thunder, the color red sometimes suffuses the screen to underscore this fear), and she makes Forio run off from the others at a full gallop, losing her hat in the process so that her hair flies out behind her.

We know Marnie knows how to jump a horse, but she does something curious in this scene. She shortens her reins, keeping the horse's head tight, so that he can't jump a stone fence properly. Here, the horse speaks: he screams at her, knowing that she is about to cause his or her own death. Astute film viewers who don't know a thing about horses frequently believe that Marnie is trying to stop Forio, having lost faith in his ability to clear that fence. But anyone who rides knows that to stop a galloping horse, one must pull back hard on both reins. Stopping Forio is not what Marnie means to do. Marnie has already tried to kill herself by drowning after the rape scene, so we know suicide remains an option (much as for Thoroughbreds, who seem to be suicides-in-waiting a lot of the time). The horse, screaming, can't make the jump and catches his back feet on the fence, throwing Marnie and falling, badly injured, himself. The pathetic, murdered horse vocalizes his pain and writhes pitifully, unable to get up. We are supposed to believe that he has broken one or more of his legs. Marnie, uninjured, gets a neighbor's gun and shoots her horse herself, instead of waiting for someone else to do it (the movie universe is still a vet-free zone). She has killed her own spirit and freedom and wildness, and she returns to Mark's familial estate to steal his money and, undoubtedly, run away with it, her default response to male authority and sexuality. Mark finds her and stages an elaborate intervention to force Marnie to face her childhood issues, and we are left with the dubious feeling that all will be well.

Forio, a beautiful black horse (black as Marnie's soul), is the only victim in the film, and with him dies Marnie's wild nature and childhood trauma. Indeed, her adoration of Forio recalls all the other little girls (and boys) who adore their horses more than anything and find in them an understanding and beauty that can't be found in humans, in this case male humans in particular. Marnie says as much: that horses are far better than humans (the only point on which I agree totally with Marnie).

No horse trainer, stuntmen, or wranglers are credited in the film. If Hitchcock had contempt for actors ("Actors should be treated like cattle," he is famous for saying), he certainly didn't care much for animals (his dispassionate dispatching of Forio is evidence), and Marnie's ability to shoot her injured horse equals Elizabeth Taylor's lack of affect at her horse being shot for a broken leg in *Giant*. I'd suggest this was because male directors and producers don't fully understand the woman-horse bond, though in Marnie's case insanity is the fundamental cause. Hitchcock did have an uncredited second unit director, William Witney, known for directing action movies with horses, such as *Zorro Rides Again* (1937) and *The Lone Ranger* (1938), and he directed the lengthy foxhunt sequence, which demanded choreographing a large group of horses and dogs; the direction of this must have been beneath Hitchcock, or Hitchcock thought he wasn't horse-smart enough: that directors have specialized assistants for such things as choreography, big musical numbers, and scenes with animals was a given.

More than this, though, was Hitchcock's method of filming Marnie riding. All of the filming was done on an enormous horse treadmill in the studio, with Tippi Hedren actually riding Forio. Background was then rear projected, and the horse appeared to be running in the country. For close-ups of Marnie on Forio riding for her life, Hitchcock borrowed a mechanical horse that the Disney Studio used for exactly the same purposes, and the mechanical horse with Hedren aboard was filmed the same way, with rear projection added.

However, someone trained Forio to lie on his side, writhing and vocalizing, after his abortive attempt to jump. The horse's scream at Marnie when she shortens his reins and his death scene are expert. Hitchcock's desire to give no credit for this great training job forces commenters on various chat sites to ask if the horse was really shot in the film, so realistic is his pain and suffering. Marnie keeps the neighbor's pistol, and the whole tragic horse episode seems to be a way to get a gun into Marnie's possession, making her all the more dangerous, truly a femme fatale.

Horses in Hitchcockland were clearly a part of affluent lifestyles, objects of luxury. Cary Grant was Hitchcock's first choice to play Mark Rutland in *Marnie*, but he was committed to another film. And Grace Kelly was the director's first choice for his leading lady, but she turned the part of Marnie down, fearing that her position as princess of Monaco didn't include in its job description playing a frigid, crazy thief. What a different film *Marnie* may have been with Grant and Kelly in darker romantic roles than in Hitchcock's charming, romantic *To Catch a Thief* (1955).

6

Magical Horses

The horse appeals to the human imagination unlike any other domesticated animal, so it's no wonder that films featuring horses with magical powers reveal the horse's super-equine abilities. In children's fairy tales, suspension of disbelief is easy for horse lovers. No other domesticated animal displays such grace, elegance, size, and beauty, a combination that creates a sense of magic and engenders, among many, fearfulness.

Beauty and the Beast (1946)

Why are magical horses nearly always white? Most movies agree on this, so it must be the case. Though I have, up until now, focused on English-language films, there is an original white horse who may have influenced the rest of the magical horses in cinema and set the standard that still exists to this day. Not to mention him would be an injustice to the history of magical horses, which surely have a unique sentience in the movies in which they appear. The foundation magical white horse appears unforgettably in French cinema in Jean Cocteau's (1889–1963) 1946 *Beauty and the Beast* (*La Belle et la Bête*) with the appropriate name Le Magnifique (the Magnificent One). And he is. He is the only means of transport, over land instead of by the instant magic of the Beast's teleporting glove, to the Beast's enchanted château and functions autonomously, as if aware of his own magical powers and jobs that he must carry out. We first see him when the Beast sends Beauty's father home from his château, cursed because he stole a rose for Beauty from the Beast's garden. The Beast's edict: either Father must return on Le Magnifique, or he must send someone in his place. The family is made up of two snooty, arrogant, utterly obnoxious older sisters, a worthless gambler of a brother, and Beauty, whom they all treat as a maid. Only she is willing to take her father's place at the Beast's château.

The first time we see Le Magnifique, in his exquisite medieval garb, his entire coat is dotted with sparkling diamonds, and one must say the magic words to him to get him to take you to the Beast: "Va, va, va, Le Magnifique. Va ou je vais," meaning, loosely translated, "Go, go, go, Le Magnifique. Go where I wish to go." Beauty rides him as a jockey would ride, flattened over his withers as if withstanding severe weather, and the big white horse moves gracefully through the woods to deliver her to her fate.

Le Magnifique adds to the magic of the Beast's environment, where statues come to life, human arms hold candelabras on the walls, and characters move in a mysterious slow motion down an endlessly windy hallway. And the ultimate magic is the Beast himself. Talk about magnificent! The makeup took hours to apply to actor Jean Marais, including an hour for each fingernail and wiggling the ears worked by a hidden operator, René Clément, via sticks. Marais owned a beloved Husky dog named Moulouk, who was the model for the Beast. With his animal head set off by a huge, standing, lace collar and exquisite medieval garb similar to his horse's (a lush costume designed by Pierre Cardin), the Beast is irresistible, his looks a walking metaphor for his troubled soul. "Never look into my eyes," he says to Beauty, as if this demonstration of dominance might cause him to lose control and murder her. The art direction is equally exquisite, based on Gustave Doré's engravings. All of this magic is enhanced by the balletic movement of the characters, frequently without any dialogue, making the magic of the château an inescapable ambience. Josette Day as Beauty personifies grace.

But the Beast and Le Magnifique are the most memorable characters; they blur the lines between what is civilized and what is wild and raise the questions of why and how one might be superior to the other. The animal world has none of the meanness of spirit that the human world encompasses. When, at the end, the Beast's life is saved and his humanity reappears, one must be disappointed. As Greta Garbo supposedly said after attending the premiere in France, "Give me back my beautiful beast." Le Magnifique, like the Beast, is a force of nature, untamed, knowing his destination without being told, needing no human to guide him. Like the Beast, he is both emotional and intelligent yet completely untamed—a dream of a horse. Cocteau made several other magical films, two about Orpheus and his foray into the underworld to rescue his dead wife, but none inspires and appeals to the child in all of us as *La Belle et le Bête* does, just as no remake of this fairy tale inspires audiences as the literally fabulous Cocteau version does in its introduction of a dreamworld made real, with the original white magical horse, diamond-encrusted, taking us to our destination.

Winter's Tale (2014) and *The Lone Ranger* (2013)

And the fabulous magical white horses turn up in some of the most wretched films, films that are otherwise nearly unwatchable. *Winter's Tale* (2014) is one of these, a film that is as bad and sappy and dull as a film can be, even one starring Colin Farrell, who has made some abysmal choices in his acting career. But the horse—what a thrilling beauty! The horse, whom Peter Lake (Farrell) calls simply Horse, becomes his guardian angel, showing up when Lake needs to escape a difficult, even potentially deadly, situation. Huge, with a long forelock flowing into its eyes, a gloriously shaggy mane reminiscent of a Mick Jagger midcareer hairdo, and conveniently bridled and reined at all times for ease of riding, this stallion outruns all difficulty, and when it can't simply outrun, it flies. Horse's wings seem made of smoke or other gossamer material, truly exquisite, and his flight is as balletic as his earthbound movement. When interviewed to promote *Winter's Tale*, Farrell testified that this Andalusian stallion (actually named Listo) created difficulty for him because the horse had less interest in filming and more interest in any mares nearby and would run off, with Farrell aboard, if the possibility of an assignation existed. Nevertheless, in the film, Horse listens to Farrell, and they are gorgeous together. This story of lost love disappears from one's mind as soon as the film is over, but Horse remains. Even the cinematography of the great Caleb Deschanel (of *The Black Stallion*), the skill of horse trainer Rex Peterson, and endless CGI crew can't save this dismal effort, written and directed by Akiva Goldsman (1962–). It's the kind of movie that makes you ask, "Did anyone direct this?"

Yet another magical white horse who finds himself mired in a dreadful production is the horse who is eventually named Silver in the 2013 version of *The Lone Ranger*. The film is a mess, which can't decide if it wants to be comedy, parody, western, or drama, with the changes in tone registering on the Richter scale, a plot that careens through badly constructed twists and turns like an out-of-control roller coaster, and truly wretched writing that gives the actors, Armie Hammer as John Reid/The Lone Ranger and Johnny Depp as Tonto, little to do aside from keeping straight faces as they utter the impossible dialogue.

But the horse! First seen on a cliff in Monument Valley (a location beloved by filmmaker John Ford, and part of the canon of the western), he rears and paws at the air, free and wild, after a posse of Texas Rangers has been ambushed by a bad guy with particularly poor personal dental hygiene. All seven are dead, including Reid and his brother, but Tonto informs us that the conveniently appearing horse is a spirit horse, able to return one of the men from the dead. To Tonto's amazement, the white horse comes to the grave site and chooses John Reid as his person, bringing with him John's enormous

The Lone Ranger, 2013. Johnny Depp as Tonto communes with Silver. Directed by Gore Verbinski. (Walt Disney Studios Motion Pictures/Photofest. ©Walt Disney Studios Motion Pictures.)

white cowboy hat. Reid, a citified lawyer, has not inspired confidence in Tonto, and he questions the horse about this choice; however, the animal remains convinced even as Tonto begs him to resurrect instead the courageous brother. Tonto talks to the horse throughout the film, and the horse looks into his eyes and snorts and whinnies back at Tonto. Throughout the film, the horse demonstrates more personality than the actors, drinking beer and burping, saving our heroes from a burning barn by leaping onto its roof ("The horse can fly?" Reid asks Tonto), eating CGI scorpions off Reid and Tonto's faces, wearing Reid's white hat, and, in a thrilling finale, galloping, with Reid in the saddle, across the rooftops of the town and then onto the top of a train escaping with Butch, the dentally challenged bad guy, and a fortune's worth of mined silver. He eventually leaps into a train car and carries on with his pursuit of Butch. The main horse used to play Silver was actually named Silver long before the film came into being (though four others also do specialty tricks) and is a Thoroughbred/Quarter Horse mix, though another white horse, Cloud, did the beer drinking, magnificent jumps off buildings, and racing across the rooftops. The iconic Lone Ranger, aboard the rearing Silver, is of course depicted here too, though Reid is chastened by Tonto for such showing off: "Don't ever do that again." Horses named Casper and Leroy also play Silver, and the head horse trainer's beloved horse Houdini, who died of colic soon after filming, plays Scout, Tonto's horse.

Bobby Lovgren (1964–) was this film's head trainer, and he was also a trainer for *War Horse* and *Seabiscuit*, as well as other films. He has to be considered the best movie horse trainer in the business because of his ability to make horses' emotions known to us. His trademark is turning his trick horses into actors. They are aware of the action going on around them and vocalize frequently to comment on it. Lovgren trained Silver to look right into the camera in his scenes, and actors talk to the horses in all three films mentioned, elevating the horse from mere vehicle for cowboys to a true character who influences the action. Because of this, Lovgren should be the most sought-after trainer in films, as his horses endear themselves to horse lovers because of their sentience. Whether or not Silver is actually a spirit horse is never in question, although throughout the film Tonto exclaims, "Something wrong with this horse!" for choosing Reid to resurrect, even to the point of telling Reid that his frequent nickname, "Kemosabe," means "wrong brother." Though these shenanigans may sound charming, truly the only charming element of the film is the magical white horse, especially now that both Hammer's and Depp's careers seem to be in freefall because of revelations, true or false, from their real lives. The director of *The Lone Ranger*, Gore Verbinski (1964–), is also known for his direction of *Pirates of the Caribbean* movies. So his trademark would appear to be chaos and questionable scripts, but he fills the screen with action in an attempt to make up for his shortcomings.

Into the West (1992)

Into the West (1992), directed by Mike Newell (1942–), of *Four Weddings and a Funeral* and *Donnie Brasco*, and written by the director of the great *My Left Foot*, Jim Sheridan (1949–), may be one of the best magical horse movies ever made. It has a terrific cast, starring the craggy Gabriel Byrne as John Riley, the embittered, alcoholic widower with two young sons and a past life as the king of the Travellers, a legendary figure reduced to being a "settler" in housing towers in Dublin; his then-wife Ellen Barkin as a wild-haired itinerant tracker; and a young Brendan Gleeson as a bad cop. However, the real star is the magical white horse, who appears at a beach where Riley's father is camped, out of nowhere (as if out of the sea), and follows the old man, with his wagon and black draft horse and wolfhound, back to the Traveller camp, where the horse instantly becomes tame in the presence of Riley's two young sons, Ossie and Tito, who jump on his back and ride him with ease, when no one else could tame him. It is another use of the right and only person for a specific horse.

At the itinerant camp, Grandfather Riley tells the boys that the horse's name is Tír na nÓg (try to pronounce that without seeing the movie!), a mythical place from Irish folklore where the inhabitants never grow old. Echoing the story of John Riley and his fall from grandeur after the death of his young wife in childbirth, the handsomest Traveller ever goes there with a princess but insists on returning, after a thousand years, to his Traveller life. The princess gives him a magical white horse whom he must not ever dismount, for if he does, he will turn to dust before the eyes of the other Travellers. The boys are in love with the horse, and the feeling is clearly mutual, as the soulful close-ups of the horse's eyes demonstrate a sentience, comprehension, and even a charted course, horse-created and moving the narrative forward, that are remarkable. Donal Fortune, the horse master, and Tony Smart, the stunt coordinator (who also worked with the horses on Ridley Scott's *Robin Hood*), must be the

Into the West, 1992. Ciarán Fitzgerald and Rúaidhrí Conroy, the two runaway Roma boys on their beloved Tír na nÓg. Directed by Mike Newell. (Miramax/ Photofest. ©Miramax.)

ultimate horse lovers. Their use of this beautiful horse is as complex as the human characters, perhaps even more so, as the horse, it turns out, is on a mysterious mission of redemption.

The film's title refers both to the traditional home of the Travellers, in western Ireland, to which the horse returns the boys on the lam, and to the boys' love of western movies, as this movie world provides escape from their poverty, their father's alcoholism, and their loss of their ancestral way of life, which should have included horses. Tír na nÓg promises a fulfillment of all their wishes, as well as a revelation the boys couldn't suspect.

When first seen, the white horse prances, with its tail up in the air—a behavior horses enjoying themselves do in reality, though in this case we must wonder if the horse's joy in being alive is due to some magic. It snorts and whinnies, rears and paws, and has a gorgeous high-kneed gait, clearly the epitome of magical white horseness. The boys ride it home and into the lobby of their tenement, into the elevator, and then into their apartment, the instinctive claustrophobia of most horses apparently not an issue for this wondrous being. When Riley is awakened in an alcoholic stupor by the horse's nuzzling, he buries his head under his pillow, believing he is hallucinating. At the Travellers' camp, where the gypsies have built a fire, the kids, on their coarse horses, dare each other to jump a small fire, and the other horses blanch at the last minute, but Tír na nÓg easily jumps it, with Ossie mounted, without hesitation. The horse accompanies the boys when they beg for change on the streets and then returns home with them for a bath in their bathroom. But a neighbor, frightened by the horse in the tenement, has called the coppers, led by Brendan Gleeson, and though the boys try to escape with the horse, they are eventually caught, and the horse is taken away after jumping an impossibly high fence before the amazed policemen. The whole time, the horse demonstrates an awareness and comprehension of its situation, the close-ups of its profound, beautiful eyes clueing the viewer in to an ability to reason, understand, and even plan.

Sold to a rich businessman by Gleeson, the horse is soon on television, now a champion jumper. Ossie and Tito see this by chance and go off into the world to recover their beloved horse, spurring police chases and Riley's own search for his sons using Traveller trackers he knows from his previous life. The boys find and steal the horse, ending up jumping a freight train with him and going on an adventure they have no control over. The horse knows where it needs to go. The three even spend a night in a closed movie theater; while they watch a movie, the horse eats popcorn and drinks punch, with Ossie talking to him the entire time. The two have a profound connection, which reaches its zenith when the horse takes the boys to their mother's grave. "Why did she die on my birthday?" Ossie asks, looking at the gravestone. We learn that their mother died in childbirth, having been turned away by a hospital because she was a Traveller. Finally we understand Riley's bottomless grief and alcoholism. This is the mission the horse has been on: revelation and an end to Riley's tragic alcoholism, for he too reaches a cathartic resolution after he is led to the grave on the trail of his boys.

But the wealthy businessman wants his champion jumping horse back, and he, in a helicopter, and the police are also tracking the horse, driving it to the sea, where Riley and the trackers are camped, truly into the west. The horse, with Ossie on him, swims into the ocean to get away, and Riley is finally spurred into action in the world of the living, as he swims after them and brings the boy back from drowning. The horse is assumed lost at sea, drowned, but is he? The film ends as the boys get a glimpse of him at the Travellers' camp, and I prefer to believe this isn't a vision but is real. Tír na nÓg is unmistakable, with his elegant, arched neck, his high-kneed stride, and those eyes that are more than human, clearly magical. Kudos too to cinematographer Newton Thomas Sigel, who is an art school graduate and began his artistic life as a painter, for his sensitive ability to create a horse as main character. This horse may be the best magical horse in film.

The Adventures of Baron Munchausen (1943 and 1988)

The saga of Baron von Munchausen began in 1785, when Rudolf Erich Rospe wrote the fantasy fiction *Baron Munchausen's Narrative of His Marvellous Travels and Campaigns in Russia* and the somewhat lecherous, mendacious, and magical hero was born. His tall tales were a natural fit for film, with George Méliès first creating a short film, *Baron Munchausen's Dream*, in 1911.

But the first full-length film of Munchausen's miraculous life has a strange history all its own, as it was made in 1943, in Germany, to celebrate the twenty-fifth anniversary of German film giant UFA (Universum-Film Aktiengesellschaft). UFA was part of Adolf Hitler and Joseph Goebbels's propaganda arm, producing pro-Nazi films that were adoring documentaries about the Third Reich in all its glory. But Goebbels had artistic pretensions, and for his film company's twenty-fifth anniversary, he wanted to demonstrate to the world that UFA could make not just propaganda but also glorious, luxurious, beautiful, funny, and magical films; thus it churned out *The Adventures of Baron Munchhausen*, which had its own kind of artistic pretension. Directed by Josef von Baky (1902–1966), it features the usual Munchausen tropes, such as him riding the cannonball, the Turkish sultan and his palace, the super-rifle, and the fastest man alive. Barely noticeable is the baron's gray steed, nameless in this account, who nevertheless understands human speech and desire. The horse vocalizes when an attractive woman bares her cleavage, echoing his master's lust, and gaining appreciation for this. The horse, though clearly sentient, never develops into a real character, with real magic. The film was remade by Monty Python member Terry Gilliam many years later.

What does it say about a film if all you remember of it is boredom and one magical white horse? It says a lot about the horse, in this case named Bucephalus (the name of Alexander the Great's mythical horse), the Baron Munchausen's steed, in Terry Gilliam's 1988 film *The Adventures of Baron Munchausen*. Trained by Tony Smart, the stunt coordinator of *Into the West*, the white horse is a dead-ringer for the one who played Tír na nÓg, though I could find no documentation that would support that. But Bucephalus does similar tricks to Tír na nÓg, such as sitting like a dog during a discussion of strategy by the human characters, and has a similar sentience. The film would have benefited from a plot, any old plot, instead of a series of picaresque adventures in a world densely inhabited by humans, creatures, and period costumes.

But Bucephalus! When the baron (played by John Neville) is about to be executed by the Turkish sultan over a wager, he whistles for his white companion, who breaks into the sultan's harem to be mounted by Munchausen and dive through a second- or third-story wall, landing effortlessly and allowing the baron to escape with his life. Bucephalus breaks into hell to rescue the baron and later rises, levitating, from the sea after escaping from that unique prison of the insides of a giant sea monster. Bucephalus vocalizes, rears, and, in battle, pirouettes like the most graceful ballet dancer, allowing the baron to slay the foes surrounding him. No wonder, as a horse lover, all I remembered was Bucephalus, a horse star in search of a plot. The humans remain forgettable, though they have charming moments. This film lost $38 million, got limited distribution (to the grief and anger of its makers), and all but disappeared. Yet Bucephalus is remembered, if only for that one heroic, impossible leap.

The Lord of the Rings: The Fellowship of the Ring (2001), *The Lord of the Rings: The Two Towers* (2002), and *The Lord of the Rings: The Return of the King* (2003)

Given the number of horse staff listed for The Lord of the Rings Trilogy (2001–2003) directed and cowritten by Peter Jackson (1961–), adapted from the classic fantasy novels by J. R. R. Tolkien, you'd think that the horses, some two hundred of them, would be among the best movie horses ever, especially the magical white horse Shadowfax, whom the wizard Gandalf (Ian McKellan) rides. Instead, we are presented with the biggest missed opportunity in horse movies, as Shadowfax, called "the lord of all horses" by Gandalf and from the breed Mearas, the wild horses of Middle Earth, isn't much more than a wizard-mobile. Certainly, he's gorgeous, a white Andalusian. Known for their elegance, intelligence, and dressage ability, Andalusians are equine nobility, tracing their heritage back to the fifteenth century in Spain and to lordly Arabians owned by the Moors, a far longer pedigree than the aristocratic Thoroughbred breed. Shadowfax is played by two Andalusian stallions, Blanco and Demero, to perfection. Gandalf rides him without saddle or bridle, as, according to the books, Shadowfax understands the language of man and clearly has a psychic bond with Gandalf, who, also according to the books, was the first man to tame and ride him. It's impressive to behold Gandalf riding Shadowfax at a full gallop, with no tack whatsoever. However, the white horse is little more than set dressing, as he demonstrates no self-awareness at all, no personality, no emotion.

Shadowfax doesn't even appear until the second part of the trilogy, *The Two Towers* (2002). When Gandalf needs him for his special speed, he whistles, and Shadowfax appears in all his incandescent glory. Later, Gandalf will say to him, "Run, Shadowfax. Show us the meaning of haste," and the horse can really go. In the third part of the trilogy, *The Return of the King* (2003), Shadowfax rears and strikes the crazy king Denethor in the head to keep him from setting his still-living son Faramir on fire on a funeral pyre. This scene was particularly difficult to film, as the horse, naturally, feared fire; so a recording of the fire was projected on a sheet of glass, allowing the horse to do his stunt without fear. Other dangerous scenes involving horses in battle were filmed with both horses and men in "motion capture" suits shot in a studio, and later inserted digitally into battle scenes. Nevertheless, it is rumored that twenty-seven horses, goats, cows, and sheep died while making the trilogy.

Viggo Mortensen, who plays Aragorn, the future king of all the realms of Middle Earth, demonstrates his profound affinity for horses in the trilogy; he even purchased three of the horses from the movies after filming, two for himself and one, the gray ridden by Arwen (Liv Tyler), for trainer and stuntwoman Jane Abbott because she had developed a great love for the horse. Mortenson's best horse scene is when he nearly has been killed, thrown into a rushing river in battle; he eventually winds up, near death, on the shore. His horse—named Brego in the film but played by a handsome bay Dutch Warmblood stallion with a star actually named Uraeus—finds him. The horse puts his nose and mouth to Mortenson's face, as if kissing him or giving him artificial respiration, and then lies down next to Mortenson so that he may pull himself onto the horse with ease. Ureaus died in 2015, much to Mortenson's dismay.

Though this film trilogy may have pleased, and even thrilled, *Lord of the Rings* devotees, to those of us uncharmed by Tolkien's writing (though loved by people who don't otherwise read) or a pure good-and-evil-fueled plot, Jackson's film makes one long for more complexity. The seemingly medieval world has no dogs, cats, rats, or mice and is spectacularly clean, a Middle Earth Switzerland. In contrast, part of what makes Mortenson so compelling as Aragorn is his endless grime and his greasy hair. Personal hygiene becomes difficult when you're fighting evil full time.

One also longs for the sensitive training of Bobby Lovgren, Rex Peterson, and Tony Smart, who seem able to train their horses to actually act and demonstrate emotion. Silver and Tír na nÓg become fleshed-out characters in *The Lone Ranger* and *Into the West*, while Shadowfax remains a beautiful, seemingly magical cipher. Perhaps Peter Jackson–world is black and white in its duality themes, its good or evil characters, and its uninteresting horses. More magic, not less, was needed to fulfill the needs of horse lovers, but the closest we get is when Brego gives Aragorn the kiss of life. Jackson, the director, has far more interest in CGI and other technical magic than in the magic of the human love affair with the horse.

7

Heartstrings

We horse lovers have a love/hate relationship with certain films that use horses to make us cry. We can watch violence being done by humans to humans in any Quentin Tarantino or Martin Scorsese film without getting weepy, but hurt or kill a horse and the flood-gates open. This phenomenon may say something important and even sinister about the nature of the horse lover's soul—we may be miscreants when it comes to humans. But our hearts are pure when it comes to horses.

The Misfits (1961) and *No Country for Old Men* (2007)

The Misfits (1961) is a film you either hate to love or love to hate. Wild horses are rounded up for profit and slaughter; although they struggle mightily against the men who would capture them, they lose their battle for their continued wild existence, their souls, their integrity. The thematic irony is that the men doing the rounding up are men deeply invested in their off-the-grid, free existence, part of a dying breed: cowboys. They are proud of their migratory, rodeo lives, and that they don't work for wages, the worst thing that can happen to a man. The point is made that in the old days, these wild mustangs were rounded up to be turned into riding horses because of their small size and endurance. But now they're sold to be turned into dog food. Their day of usefulness has passed, as has the cowboys'. What makes the film more tragic are Clark Gable's death, which occurred less than two weeks after filming was completed; Marilyn Monroe's premature and mysterious demise; and the premature passing of Montgomery Clift in 1966, the result of alcoholism and drug addiction.

The film is about real, human death, horse death, and the death of cultures of freedom, and it has a sepulchral quality that informs every frame—not to mention its purple pedigree: it was written by Arthur Miller (then married to Marilyn Monroe) and directed by John Huston. David Niven fully believes, as detailed in one of his memoirs, that *The Misfits* killed Gable, the true professional on set, having to put up with Monroe's and Clift's epic lateness and lack of preparedness. Bored by the endless waiting, Gable insisted on doing many of his own stunts with the wild horses in the extreme desert heat, and this took its toll on his already fragile heart. Gable, in real life, was part of that dying breed of true professionals, there to do a day's work. The son he had long wanted wasn't born until shortly after his death.

But the horses in *The Misfits* aren't merely symbols. The stallion who leads the small band of wild mustang mares struggles mightily with Gable, Clift, and Eli Wallach, refusing to be tamed until the three men wear him down with their efforts. Like his herd, the stallion is left pitifully tied up to a truck tire in the desert outside of Reno, Nevada, awaiting the dealer who will pick them all up (how he'd get them into a trailer for transport in this middle-of-nowhere desert is beyond me). When Clift, suddenly comprehending Monroe's empathy for these beautiful wild creatures, cuts his rope to set him free, the stallion engages in yet another clash with Gable, a kind of macho bout for alpha male. Gable is dragged by the stallion, who then rears and paws at him, seemingly about to kill him, but Gable subdues him, pets him, and then sets him free. Gable's character, Gay Langford, has had an epiphany like that of Clift's character,

Perce Howland, and he frees all the horses. Do they now realize that the animals they struggle with are the equine versions of themselves?

Miller based Monroe's character, Roslyn Taber, on Monroe's actual life, specifically her sorry childhood in foster homes and orphanages. If Monroe off the soundstage was half as empathic and compassionate as this character, she was indeed a rare individual. She feels for these damaged men, Gay's dog Tom Dooley, and especially for the horses and their ugly fate, though she is also a sexual object desired by all of the male characters. At thirty-five, Monroe's face appears puffy and, in some shots, lined, and her waistline has thickened. But like the wild horses, she has ineffable, untamable qualities which are unmistakable. Her soon-to-be ex-husband Miller wrote this film as a love letter to her, her sweetness and her impossibility in the real world. So she too is twinned with the wild horses, not long for this ugly world.

Gable too appears weather-beaten and past his prime, though he gives an amazing performance as Gay, and Clift, who had suffered a nearly fatal car accident in 1957, has a face with no memory of his fine, good looks before that accident, not unlike the wild horses, who are thin and rugged and as opposite of well-cared-for Thoroughbreds and show horses as billionaires are from homeless people. In these three stars, the casting is brilliant, though profoundly troubling. Nearly everything about this film is disconcerting. This is a tragic and romantic film (Percy Bysshe Shelley's "Ode to the West Wind" comes to mind: "A heavy weight of hours has tamed and bowed one too like thee/tameless and swift and proud," and Shelley may even be the inspiration for Clift's character's name, Perce) in which neither cowboys nor wild horses can truly fit into the modern world nor can men and women truly connect or fit together to find happiness. Thelma Ritter, as Monroe's friend, says, "Cowboys are the last real men left in the world," but like the wild horses, they are a dying breed and are now misfits. Gay and the mustang stallion have no place in 1960 Reno, Nevada, and are doomed, belonging to a bygone era that has already, in the film, disappeared, though they cling to it as if it's still a reality. "Nothing can live unless something dies," Gay says, and indeed, the whole film seems a parade of death and near death.

A similar theme, of discordance between the modern world full of death and strangeness and a past world of honor and simplicity, exists in the Coen brothers' fine film *No Country for Old Men* (2007). The old world order made sense, and people behaved in a responsible fashion; those who didn't were complete outcasts. But in the present time of the film, even crime has changed, thanks to drugs and automatic weapons, and is so unflinchingly brutal that the old sheriff (Tommy Lee Jones) can only shake his head at both situations he must confront and articles he reads detailing crimes in the newspaper. While everyone else takes four-wheel-drive vehicles out to inspect a horrific murder scene where a drug deal has gone very bad, the sheriff and his deputy ride horses to it, with special care paid to his wife's horse, Winston, whom she adores. The state of the modern world is decried in many scenes (kids with green hair and bones in their noses on the streets of Texas, a murderer about to be executed who says he'd gladly do it again) and is at odds with the world the marshal wishes would come back, though it does so only in his dreams. The horses serve much the same purpose as in *The Misfits*, symbols of a better and simpler time, a means of transport that allows you to commune with another sentient species as opposed to riding in a mechanical truck. In both films, the horses represent the lost soul of a soulless present.

So although the horses in *The Misfits*, so similar to the horses in *No Country*, except for the primal stallion, don't have personalities of their own, they are the engine that moves the plot, and the metaphor that informs the plot. Their very being, wild and untamed, gives the film its tragic subtext, and they are moving beyond belief. The horse master of *The Misfits* was Friedrich von Lebedur, an excellent rider who served in the Austrian cavalry during World War I and formed a friendship with similar adventurer and raconteur John Huston (the film's director), for whom he acted in *Moby Dick* (1956) and trained horses in *The Misfits*.

The scion of a noble family, the very tall, severe-looking Lebedur surely had many tales to share with Huston, and his love and understanding of horses is evident in this movie. Huston (1906–1987) was himself a creature from another time, given to epic bouts of drinking and fisticuffs, famously once with Errol Flynn when a hoity-toity dinner party both attended became way too dull. Paradoxically a serious scholar and intellectual who could recite reams of poetry, Huston was one of the dying breed of men's men, like the Gable character in *The Misfits*. One can see traces of Huston's masculine filmmaking in *No Country*, nearly completely devoid of female characters except for those with the purpose of being wife and mother, and with its ethic of taking life without concern, as if it were a normal job.

War Horse (2011)

Horse lovers the world over wept their way through Steven Spielberg's 2011 film *War Horse*, as the travails that befall the star horse, Joey, in World War I never cease. Based on a novel (1982) of the same name by Michael Morpurgo and the hit British play (2008) written by Nick Stafford (also based on the novel), the film, like the novel, attempts to tell the story through the horse's point of view. Indeed, Joey is the main character of the film, which is a kind of horse picaresque with a varied cast of human characters, first in Devon, England, and then in France at the Battle of the Somme, with the German and British armies, and with stops at a bucolic French farm where Joey is loved by a sickly farm girl.

It is impossible not to love Joey, as he is simply a great horse, so full of emotion he deserved a Best Actor Oscar nomination. I remember reading a fan theory about Joey when the film first came out—it hypothesized that Joey was a jinx (if not Satan incarnate) and that anyone who loved him was utterly doomed. There is some truth to this—Albert, the boy who first trains him, ends up briefly blinded in the war; a young cavalry officer is killed riding him into battle for the very first time; and Joey's equine friend, Topthorn, perishes from the exigencies of wartime. Joey's superior survival skills seem to have an inverse effect on those around him, who simply cannot or do not survive. Albert (Jeremy Irvine) cherishes his father's regimental pennant from the Boer Wars and ties it to Joey's saddle when Joey joins the army, and it seems that this pennant, rather than the horse, may be accursed—everyone who touches it seems to die.

Joey is a kind of superhorse. Plow a whole rocky field to save the old homestead for Albert's father? No problem. Ride full speed into battle with explosions all around? A day at the beach. Pull ambulances full of suffering young soldiers through war-torn Europe? Easy deal. Pull German heavy artillery to the point of exhaustion and near death? Why not. If I owned Joey, he'd be painting my house and cooking me dinner. I was a sucker for Joey—how could a horse lover not be? Horse owners frequently anthropomorphize their favorite horses, and Joey is more human in terms of intelligence and feeling than most of the human characters.

Joey was played by numerous real, mechanical, and CGI horses. Horse lovers will be pleased to know that the scene of Joey pathetically trapped in barbed wire featured an animatronic horse rather than a real one, and that scene is the epitome of pathos when a German soldier and an American soldier both leave their trenches to work together to save the trapped horse, a brief peace treaty based on the love of horses.

This film employed an army of various types of technicians, and the management of the equines offers more credits than on any other film I've seen. There is a second unit equine director, Tom Rye; an artistic equine adviser, Alexandra Bannister; an equine supervisor, Robert Grayson; multiple horse trainers; and stuntmen galore, as well as an on-set veterinarian. But the name that stands out is that of Bobby Lovgren, the horse master, perhaps the very best horseman when it comes to making horses into sentient characters. The heartstrings that are pulled in *War Horse* are plucked by Lovgren, a phenomenal choice by director Spielberg (1946–) to ensure a weeping audience for poor Joey.

There are the usual horse issues in the film that are irksome, similar to those in *Secretariat* (2010). At the beginning of the film, Joey's mother is in the process of foaling on a sunny day in verdant Devon. She lives in a huge meadow, but she is polite enough to foal within sight of the fence, with two men able to attend to her. In real horse life, a mare would head to the far end of that meadow to foal, utilizing her survival instincts to protect the newborn from predators, and she would foal in the dead of night, again for protection, because by daylight the foal would be standing, nursing, and ready to move with its herd. But Joey's mum is very English, polite and untroubling to her owners. Young Albert, a neighbor, is there to behold this scene as well, leaning on the convenient fence.

Similarly, weaning Joey from his dam is way too easy. Anyone who has ever weaned a horse knows that both the foal and the mare go completely insane and attempt to hurt themselves and the humans involved. Weaning is one of the most dangerous things one does with horses, and the crying and fence-running are ceaseless. Young Joey is led away from his mother with only a couple of minor escape attempts controlled only by a rope halter and rope lead, sold at auction to Albert's father, and moves on with his life. Perhaps this is simply more evidence of Joey's emotional superiority and comprehension of his life, but having weaned innumerable foals from their moms, I have come to see murder/suicide attempts as the norm.

When Joey's friend from the English cavalry Topthorn, a glorious, huge black stallion, dies from exhaustion after being forced to pull German heavy artillery, Joey's response, as shown in his big, sad eyes, is tragic. He paws at Topthorn, something I have witnessed horses do to their dead friends and mares do to their stillborn foals, as if trying to get them to stand up and live again. This is heartrending to behold, in real life and in the film. I guarantee there was not a dry eye in theaters.

Another great, already described scene involves Joey making a temporary peace between England and Germany. We need him at the United Nations. Having escaped the German army, Joey has become entangled in barbed wire between English and German trenches and is suffering and unable to stand and free himself. An English soldier, holding a white flag, risks his life to attempt to free the horse, as does a German soldier who brings wire cutters; together they free Joey and then flip a coin to see who gets to take him home. Both agree that this is a remarkable horse, deserving of a better life. The Great War has stopped, for a few moments, because Joey's superior, sentient qualities are recognized, and he makes armed, warring humans better too.

More than four million horses perished in World War I, and it seemingly took almost this many horses to make *War Horse*. In the cavalry charge scenes, over 280 horses were used, and Joey was played by 14 different horses, each chosen for its unique ability to portray emotion (supplied by The Devil's Horsemen group, which will be discussed later because of the horse movie industry's dependence on it). Horse master extraordinaire Bobby Lovgren even used his own horse Finder, a *Seabiscuit* graduate, to portray the sadness of Joey at the death of his only equine friend. Four different horses played Topthorn, who was called on to display exhaustion, limping, and dying before our eyes and Joey's. Because finding horses that looked exactly like Joey and Topthorn was impossible, a huge army of equine makeup artists and equine hair stylists were employed on the film, not to mention a horde of stuntmen (there was even a goose trainer, but that's another story). As well, though animatronic and CGI horses were utilized in the barbed wire scenes, when a real horse was needed and used, the barbed wire was actually soft plastic. In small roles, a prestardom Tom Hiddleston and pre-Sherlock Benedict Cumberbatch turn up, but they are no more than supporting actors in Joey's story.

Usually, I dislike Spielberg's films, finding them emotionally shallow, melodramatic, and immature, going for cheap plucking at one's heartstrings and floundering when aspiring to something more profound. But it is impossible to dislike *War Horse*, especially if you are a horse lover and have had close relationships with certain special horses, as Albert has with Joey. There certainly can exist a profound bond between human and horse. Young Albert training young Joey is especially moving, as the former reasons with the latter and explains things to him, and the horse understands. Joey may be the ultimate horse-weeper hero, and the choice to make the film from his point of view gives it depth and meaning.

Black Beauty (1946 and 1994)

Anna Sewell (1820–1878) published her novel *Black Beauty* in 1877 to phenomenal results and bestsellerdom, which she didn't live long enough to enjoy, but it is considered to be the first novel written from the point of view of an animal, its equine main character, and to address the topic of cruelty to horses, then an epidemic in England. She thought the best way to address this issue, which was profoundly moving to her, was using Black Beauty's own narration to tell his story. Due to an accident when she was a child, she was unable to walk and therefore clearly never rode, but she took great pleasure in her father's horses and in driving him in his carriage to the railroad station where he caught the train to work daily. She set about learning all she could about horses, and was appalled at their treatment in her culture. This book came out just when film was in its embryonic form, and it was an easy fit for filming, as horses were among the first stars of motion pictures. As well, it marked the beginning of animal rights activism and caused laws to be passed in England to protect carriage horses and cab horses from cruel practices, such as the "bearing rein" or "check-rein," which forced carriage horses to carry their heads very high to create the elegant stance and gait that pleased their aristocratic owners but was utterly unnatural and caused neck, back, and leg issues for these horses, frequently leaving them crippled and useless except for the most basic jobs. As well, cab horses had always worked seven days a week, but new legislation mandated that horse cabs couldn't work on Sundays, giving both the drivers, who made a pittance, and their overworked horses a day off.

This thanks to a woman whose love of horses must have soothed her troubled, painful life.

Black Beauty has been adapted into eight films, both animated and live action, as well as numerous television series, but most of the adaptations mangle the plot of the original novel in attempts to turn it into a girl-and-horse weeper, the most common form of the horse movie genre; most are melodramatic and sentimental and in no way reflect Sewell's interest in getting the horse behavior and information correct. The 1946 adaptation, directed by Max Nosseck (1902–1972), a German expatriate, manages to be both aggravating and charming at the same time because of the elements of the plot it alters and its lack of horse knowledge. This should be a story about life seen through the eyes of a horse instead of a girl-and-horse weeper.

The film's focus becomes Anne (Mona Freeman), the daughter of English aristocracy, although she has no English accent; perhaps this is why her widowed father treats her so badly, as he clearly has disdain for Americans. Anne, we are told, is as dreamy and unfocused as Roddy McDowall's Ken in *My Friend Flicka*, and her father chides her to focus, wants her to go away to finishing school to learn how to be a proper lady rather than a tomboy, and forbids her to ever ride the mare Duchess again (the film also has shades of nascent feminism, as seen in *National Velvet*). However, Duchess foals on Anne's birthday, and Squire Wendon, Anne's father, gives her the beautiful black foal as a birthday present, warning her that she alone is responsible for the proper upbringing and disciplining of the colt. Anne, of course, is instantly in love.

Black Beauty is played by the gorgeous American Saddlebred horse Highland Dale, previously discussed as a star of many horse movies. The American Saddlebred is a cross of horse breeds dating back to 1706, when imported Thoroughbreds were crossed with native Narragansett Pacers (the first breed to be created in North America and now extinct) to bring into being a great riding horse with more elegance than the native horses, which were rather

coarse. The McCutcheon name is legendary in Texas horse country for breeding top cutting and cattle horses (Quarter Horses), and
McCutcheon made his mark in Hollywood because of Highland
Dale, who also played Elizabeth Taylor's horse in *Giant*, the main
character in *Gypsy Colt* (1954), and Broadway Bill in Frank Capra's
remake of that film, *Riding High*. He also starred in television series
Bonanza (1959–1973), *The High Chaparral* (1967–1971), and *Fury*
(1955–1960), as well as in many other roles, and earned numerous
PATSY Awards, the animal equivalent of the Oscar. It is rumored
that Highland Dale earned more than $700,000 for McCutcheon
during his career, a veritable fortune in the forties and fifties.
Highland Dale was a cottage industry for his owner, and worked up
until the time of his death.

Highland Dale is without question the best actor in the motion
picture, while human actors—especially Mona Freeman, whose voice
is always pleading and annoying, and Richard Denning, who plays
Bill Dixon, the visiting American with whom Anne falls in love—
deliver the so-super-sincere-they're-phony line readings common at
the time. Of course, this film version of *Black Beauty* must be turned
into a love story, with young Anne smitten with Bill, although he is
interested in Anne's elegant neighbor almost as much as he is interested in horses. He meets Anne when she's still a young teenager,
clearly an inappropriate match, but there's a too-sincere spark that
flickers between them that eventually influences Anne to go to finishing school, leaving her beloved Black Beauty behind, to become as
ladylike and charming as the neighbor she's so jealous of.

The first thing Black Beauty does after being born is vocalize.
Joe, the stable hand, talks to Beauty, and Beauty answers. When
Anne leaves for finishing school, Beauty, with limpid eyes, neighs
goodbye to her. Beauty has an awareness and understanding of everything going on around him; when Anne is thrown by the mare Ginger, Beauty's eyes widen in alarm, and he nickers. As a weanling, he
demonstrates his love for Anne by resting his head on her shoulder, a
very touching and realistic way that horses show affection. Highland

Dale demonstrates every emotion one can imagine a horse having and more. Beauty's first bridling is mildly difficult, but his first saddling and first ride with Anne are ridiculously easy. As someone who has taken part in the breaking of horses, I know that even the most tame and lovable of them will turn into whirling dervishes when first saddled and mounted and will usually behave even worse the second time, when they know what's coming. But Beauty is instantly "broke" and ready to go out into the world on long rides with Anne.

At this point, it is worth returning to the novel itself, as the aforementioned film really has little of the beautiful spirit of the book remaining in it. The novel is narrated by Black Beauty himself, whose emotions are more profound than any humans in the book (save Jerry Barker, the genuinely good and earnest cab driver with whom Beauty lives happily for years). Beauty uses every horse vocalization in attempts to communicate with humans, who are beyond dense, and with other horses: he and the other horses whinny, snort, and neigh, frequently with various emotions attached, such as joy, fear, and delight. But not only this. The horses can actually speak with one another, quite eloquently, and they share their past horrors with a terrible, matter-of-fact manner that communicates how the race of horses has come to expect injury, disappointment, terror, and pain at the hands of man. They articulate what it is like to be a war horse in the Crimean War; a "job horse" rented out to unknowing, ignorant, would-be horse people who handle them roughly; a cab horse, at the mercy of its poorly paid human cab driver; a hauling horse, forced to pull overloaded wagons of goods through the crowded streets of London; and a carriage horse for aristocrats, a seemingly good gig except for the demands of fashion, with horses forced into injurious postures because of the need to hold their heads way too high and to wear blinkers, which limit the horses' excellent vision and make them near-blind at night. The novel is full of lessons about the benefits of using kindness rather than cruelty and of treating animals with respect rather than thoughtlessly; the novel also stresses that the human race comes in a many-lengths second in generosity of spirit compared to horses. Men are too quick to use the whip and too slow to try to understand these articulate and emotional animals. Sewell's point of view is clear, and I'm certain that most people who love horses would agree with it completely. Anyone who has had a horse communicate something to her, whether it's the stomachache of colic or the foot pain of a developing abscess, knows that if you only listen, horses do indeed talk.

All of this is important to keep in mind when considering the 1994 movie version of *Black Beauty*, which respects and follows the plot and the spirit of Sewell's novel and adds to it the cinematographic beauty of nature and horses that men take for granted. Directed by Caroline Thompson (1956–), it is a film of fastidious and beautiful detail; what a shame that Thompson only directed one other film, *Buddy* (1997), about a woman who decides to raise a baby gorilla as part of her family. Thompson was the author of novels and numerous screenplays, including that of *Edward Scissorhands* (1990) and others for director Tim Burton, and is clearly a great lover of animals. It shows.

The dramatic and moving opening scene shows Black Beauty's birth, and it is indeed a real foaling, completely recorded. To film this realistically, the movie set had a barn full of pregnant mares likely to foal around the time they needed and who were likely to have black foals. When one did foal, she had an appropriately black foal, but without Beauty's signature white star on his forehead. Luckily a quick-witted crew member (can that crew member be Victoria Jamison, who is listed as "equine makeup" in the credits?) who doubled as a foaling hand dipped his or her fingers in white paint and daubed it onto the foal's forehead: Black Beauty was born. In the film, the good man Farmer Grey (Sean Bean—who wouldn't trust him to foal out a mare, with his utterly sincere face) brings Black Beauty lovingly into this world, appropriately at night, unlike the ridiculous daytime, peaceful meadow birth of Flicka in *My Friend Flicka* and of Joey in *War Horse*. He gets the baby up and nursing, and his broad smile demonstrates his love of horses. Having foaled more babies than

I can remember, the realism here is stunning. First the sac appears, then the nose and front feet of the baby and, with some careful, gentle pulling, Beauty is born: a textbook birth. The foal vocalizes from the start, and scenes of his early life, as he becomes aware of insects in the grass and of his mother's instructions and frolics around her, are also utterly realistic and quite beautiful thanks to the cinematography by Alex Thomson, who also created the exquisite photography in Ridley Scott's *Legend*. The film retains the conceit of first-person narration by Black Beauty himself, brought to life through his own voice.

This magnificent portrayal of the adult Black Beauty is thanks to Docs Keepin Time (1987–2013), an American Quarter Horse bred for racing but utterly untalented in that venue. He was a son of a California stallion, Merridoc, out of the TimetoThinkrich mare Sister Steph, and was coal black; Beauty's requisite star and hind sock had to be applied by makeup people. Lucky for Docs Keepin Time, trainer extraordinaire Rex Peterson (1954–), who trained the horses in *The Horse Whisperer* and *Dreamer*, among many others, found him and recognized something special in him, training him to do any trick you can imagine and naming him Justin because he found him "just in" time for filming *Black Beauty*. Justin raced twice at three and ran last and second-to-last, so his owners/breeders gave up on him, sold him, and completely lost track of him. Justin did much of his work at liberty, that is, without any kind of constraint, such as rider, halter, or lead rope. Peterson would give him verbal or physical clues, and the horse would rear, bow, lie down, sit up, nudge a ball with his nose, kiss, nod, or shake his head. Because Justin had so much to do in the film, a stunt double black horse was utilized for unusually fast or athletic work. Justin had starred for a year in a TV series, *The Adventures of the Black Stallion* (1990–1993), before flying to England with Peterson for the film and won the coveted American Quarter Horse Association's Silver Spur Award, another version of the equine Oscar.

Also on stunts was Tony Smart (1949–), who himself became a first-rate trainer as documented in *Into the West* and *The Adventures of Baron Munchausen.* Both Tony Smart and Rex Peterson find the humanity and emotional truth in horses, which was so very appropriate and necessary for *Black Beauty.*

The plot of the movie remains faithful to the novel, with the important equine characters Ginger, a victim of prior abuse thanks to which she remains unable to control her temper with humans, and Merrylegs, the white pony with a strong character and patience, who nonetheless finds it necessary to buck off the young aristocratic scion who abuses him. Black Beauty endures much abuse at the hands of various owners, as well as kindness from far fewer, and the requisite barn fire and illness occur. The horse portrayals and treatments are, however, much more realistic than in most films, beginning with that marvelous foaling. Halter-breaking isn't an easy deal, though Farmer Gray uses an excellent trick to get the halter on Beauty initially: he holds the halter in front of Beauty's head with one hand while holding a handful of oats in the other, just under the halter, so that Beauty must slip his head into the halter to get the treat. Wish I'd thought of that: it would've been useful for haltering difficult babies and for those rare horses who seem to grow fingers and remove their own halters when nobody is looking.

Beauty's first shoeing is also realistic, with the young horse lifting his front feet high in a prancing gait until he can get used to the weight of the shoes and the new feel of his feet hitting the ground. I too have seen this in newly shod yearlings. Horses are unusually sensitive about their feet, as if they understand that, as a prey species, their hooves are their only weapon against predators and running away their only strategy. When Beauty becomes ill after his misadventure with the stable lad's handling of him, medicine is realistically tubed down his throat with an ancient funnel, acknowledging that horses will not take medicine willingly and will, in fact, attempt to spit medication back on you if it is not gotten down their throats. My work clothes from the farm attest to this, with oily stains from Regu-Mate and red stains from rifampin (the only medication for a certain type of foal pneumonia, unfortunately). I could have used that antique funnel!

Beauty and the other horses in the film seem as emotional as any human and yet are also true horses. When Beauty, the new guy, is let out into the colts' paddock with the others, they all squeal and romp, kicking playfully, until Beauty is accepted as a member of that herd. Beauty paws, shakes his head, rears, and expresses himself with body language in general, as well as vocalizing. Of course, there are the requisite limpid eye close-ups, each one full of emotion, which predictably the coarse humans fail to recognize.

Thanks to Anna Sewell's novel based on horse sentience, this movie accurately captures the spirit of Sewell's titular horse, his intelligence, his emotions, his thoughts, his voice. In many ways, this film best exemplifies my desire to find movie horses with intelligence and emotion, which, from my own experience, I know they have. It is a beautiful film, and don't fear, Beauty doesn't die in the end.

8

Kevin Costner and Other Hunks on Horses

Is there anything hotter than watching a good-looking man ride a gorgeous horse with ease and expertise? For horse girls, the answer must be no. Seeing man and beast as one and man in control of the powerful beast magically makes the man that much more attractive. In that arena, the horse needs no help and merely needs to keep from killing the man in question. And if the horse girl in question knows the horse is dangerous yet is still mastered by the hunk, even better. This is an absolute rule in horse movies.

Dances with Wolves (1990)

There's a whole genre of horse lovers' movies that feature thrilling riding by an actor on a wonderful horse, though the movies may be as thrilling as watching golf. The exemplar of this concept is Kevin Costner's (1955–) *Dances with Wolves* (1990, directed by its star, frequently a terrible mistake), which was as soporific as a valium downed with a martini, except for the scenes in which he rides (and except for Wes Studi's magnificent face). That man can really ride; he's a natural. His oneness with his horse is evident throughout—and the horse! Cisco, the little dun Quarter Horse with the dorsal stripe, created a firestorm in Texas, where I then lived—every man, woman and child wanted a dun with a dorsal stripe (a darker stripe down the center of his back, very decorative) after that film came out. The owner of a Dallas arena football team bought the actual horse (really named Justin) and used him as a mascot—a prime example of someone having more dollars than sense. Put Costner on Cisco and have them traverse gorgeous countryside, adding in buffalo and wolves and Native Americans, and you've got Oscar gold.

Cisco is like a homing pigeon in *Dances with Wolves*, and despite numerous attempts to steal him, he always comes home to Dunbar (Costner), a demonstration of doglike loyalty. They are a perfect match. Trained by head trainer, head wrangler, and stunt designer Rusty Hendrickson (1953–), Cisco has more personality and verve than his rider, whose low-key presence and uninflected voice unfortunately dampen the film. The Native Americans portrayed in the film, on the other hand, have magnificent faces that brim with life, especially the aforementioned Wes Studi and Rodney A. Grant, whose visages belong on a coin. White people in general in this narrative are sorry, mean, faded versions of humanity, willing to kill both Cisco and Two Socks, Dunbar's wolf, for no other reasons than that they own guns that demand to be fired and animal life must be ended to enhance their own paltry life force. The problem, of course, is that Dunbar is one of them, a pale imitation of the vitality of the Indians, making Cisco and Two Socks completely lovable while Dunbar remains a phantom.

There is a Costner signature stunt in *Dances with Wolves*, though, that amazes anyone who has ever ridden a horse, and, one hopes, those who haven't. At the film's opening, Dunbar, a lieutenant in the Union army during the Civil War, has been gravely wounded and exhausted doctors take a coffee break before amputating his foot. Dunbar rouses himself, pulls on his boot, and stumbles out to steal a horse, Cisco, and ride out before the Confederate line in attempted suicide. Cisco and Dunbar cross the entire line of shooters unscathed, the little horse galloping for his life. But Dunbar's face shows his disappointment, and he turns to ride back. This time, though, Christlike, he raises his arms up and out and rides reinless, wildly galloping, eyes shut. This rouses the Union side, previously downcast and without hope, to victory. Riding a galloping horse is a difficult balancing act, with most untutored humans able to only hang on for dear life, but Costner remains motionless and balanced on Cisco, his long legs gripping the horse's barrel, a perfect melding of man and horse.

In the most famous and compelling scene of the film, the buffalo hunt, Costner repeats this riding motif, this time not riding toward his own death but instead riding through a huge herd of buffalos, hunting with his Sioux friends. He rides without reins, at furious speed, both hands on his rifle to shoot and kill the beasts. Viewers may forget to breathe during this sequence, which involved real buffalo, mechanical buffalo, buffalo trainers, and buffalo wranglers. One can only marvel at Costner's ability (and in most of the hunt, it is clearly Costner and not a stunt double riding) and at Hendrickson's ability to choreograph such a chaotic scene to perfection. *Dances with Wolves* is well worth seeing for Costner's oneness with the adorable Cisco, not to mention the plethora of Indian ponies and other horses: hundreds of them. The movie is horse heaven.

Silverado (1985)

Less soporific, even to those who don't love westerns, is *Silverado* (1985), which is basically *The Big Chill* (1983) on horseback—what could be bad? In fact, *The Big Chill* was expected to be Costner's breakthrough role, as the dead friend in flashbacks, but he ended up on director Lawrence Kasdan's cutting room floor. Director-writer Kasdan (1949–) was at the helm of both films, and Costner playing the dead friend for whom the old buddies gather to mourn in *Chill* is simply the friend's corpse. Kevin Costner has a terrific little paint horse in *Silverado* and gets to leap onto him from every angle, showing off his thrilling riding skills in a funny, kinetic performance that gives no hint of the self-serious, stone-faced Costner of the future. This

Costner had fun, especially on his little pinto. We see a running mount by Costner after his jailbreak as well as bareback riding, but the best is Costner's signature stunt, when he rides bareback, reins dropped, shooting his pistols with both hands. There are many scenes in which all of the principles ride together: Klein on his handsome, white-faced bay, Scott Glenn on his gray, and Danny Glover on his Wayne-worthy chestnut with a star, strip, and socks. But that trio bounces in their saddles. I'm sure they all had sore rear ends at the closing of shooting every day. Costner, on the other hand, rides as if he's a centaur, part of his adorable pinto. The film even acknowledges his ability when, toward the end, Costner winds up kidnapped by the bad guys. His also-kidnapped nephew tells Scott Glenn that the Costner character is dead, having fallen off his horse going over a cliff while trying to escape. Glenn says with incredulity and mischief, "Jake fell off his horse?" We know that Jake will reappear to save the day.

But Kevin Kline has a horse he adores and even shares passionate kisses with in a scene that is unforgettable if you love horses—it is Kline's reunion with his beloved horse after it has been stolen. When asked to prove that the horse is his, Kline says, "This horse loves me," and it certainly does. The horse gently mouths Kline's face when they are reunited, in a love scene for the ages (reminiscent of a hilarious scene from the 1941 screwball comedy *The Lady Eve*, in which a horse makes unwelcome advances to Henry Fonda while he's trying to woo Barbara Stanwyck). Luckily for Kline, he has also carved his name into his saddle, because the corrupt sheriff, as always played by Brian Dennehy who chews scenery for breakfast, isn't convinced. Anyone who has ever loved a horse, however, is convinced. All I can figure is that Kline's face must've been rubbed with peppermint oil to achieve this trick, as I have been licked and hugged by my favorite horses but have never been offered such a make-out session. Corky Randall (1929–2009), credited as "livestock ramrod," was an ace horse trainer who had a bevy of stuntmen to carry out his horse tricks in *Silverado*, with first names such as Tex, Whitey, and Autry: sometimes, names can be destiny.

Hidalgo (2004)

Another man who can really ride is Viggo Mortensen (1958–), and he demonstrates that in the film *Hidalgo* (2004), with horse master Joel Proust, who went on to work with Ridley Scott, as did the stunt coordinator, Ricardo Cruz Jr., and head horse trainer, Rex Peterson—quite the assemblage of horse expertise in *Hidalgo*. Mortensen plays a cowboy in a Wild West show, the real-life cowboy and con man Frank T. Hopkins; he rides an aging but handsome pinto with personality and smarts to spare. Invited by an Arabic potentate to take part in an epic endurance race with an equally epic purse for the winner, Mortensen decides to have one last adventure with Hidalgo. Like movie star Kevin Costner, Mortensen can really wrap those long legs around a horse, and his ease in the saddle equals Costner's as well. The addition of the chin dimple doesn't hurt, either. Also, there is something clearly magical about paint horses. They make a decorative addition to any film and have a stuffed-animal quality about them. Mortensen, who grew up in Venezuela and Argentina, where he undoubtedly learned his riding skills, matches Costner by riding Hidalgo bareback across the finish line of the desert endurance race.

Hidalgo, the eponymous pony, was played by numerous horses, and Mortenson ended up buying his favorite of them, a registered paint named FH Tecontender, while the screenwriter, John Fusco, bought the main stunt horse playing the titular Hidalgo and retired him to his own Indian horse conservancy ranch. The horse who enacted most of Hidalgo's scenes had been owned by the head horse trainer, Rex Peterson, since he was three years old. The main actor, Hidalgo, only 14.2 hands tall, is a great actor. He has numerous reaction scenes to human foibles, and the intelligence in his eyes is remarkable. He does double takes, vocalizes, comes to Mortensen when whistled for, drags a drunk Mortenson over dusty ground in the "Wounded Soldier Trick," and has numerous conversations with Mortensen, who gets to utter the immortal line, "Nobody hurts my horse," when Hidalgo suffers a horrible injury due to a trap set for

Hidalgo, 2004. Viggo Mortensen rides Hidalgo in a never-ending race. Directed by Joe Johnston. (Buena Vista Pictures/Touchstone Pictures/Photofest. ©Buena Vista Pictures/Touchstone Pictures. Photographer: Richard Cartwright.)

him. Hidalgo may be the best movie horse ever—his bond with Mortensen and his acting ability make him irresistible.

Another noteworthy horse in *Hidalgo* is the coal-black Arabian stallion, Al-Hataal, who is utter perfection and supposedly the epitome of good breeding. He is glorious. The only issue with horses in the film is that the monochromatic Arabians are undaunted by the appearance among their ranks of a spotted horse. I once boarded a paint horse for a short time for a client, and when I turned it out into a small paddock adjacent to my mare paddock, my Thoroughbred monochromatic horses went crazy, terrified by the spotted pony. I've also had Thoroughbred mares go nuts at the sight of my farrier's spotted standard poodle. Horses have a profound belief that animals should manifest only a predominant color, but the Arabians in *Hidalgo* have no response to this alien in their midst.

Hollywood must be taken to task for its all-too-frequent use of the "based on a true story" citing at the beginning of films. Hidalgo is one such film. Aside from the fact that no "true story" can be made to fit into the watch works of the screenplay form, the story of Frank T. Hopkins (1865–1951) has long been disputed by historians of the old West, despite screenwriter Fusco's claims of absolute adherence to the true story. Hopkins claimed to have ridden in over four hundred endurance races, to have introduced trick riding to Wild Bill Cody's Wild West Show, and to have been a buffalo hunter, Indian fighter, African explorer, big game guide, secret agent, and Pinkerton agent. He also claimed to be the son of the only survivor of Custer's Last Stand at the Little Big Horn and a Lakota Sioux woman, hence the thematic twinning in the film of Hopkins, of mixed breed, and Hidalgo, a lowly bred pinto, pitted against the centuries of pure breeding of the Arabian horses engaged in the (mythical) endurance race Hopkins claimed to have won. In reality, most historians say, Hopkins worked as a horse handler for the Ringling Brothers Circus, dug subway tunnels in Philadelphia, and engaged in epic mendacity to produce his own legend. But does any of this matter in terms of the film? Not to me. The cowboy code of honor and truth doesn't apply to filmmaking or to the adorableness of Hidalgo. Viggo does ride again, in the 2008 film *Appaloosa*, directed by and also starring Ed Harris; it is a far lesser movie, although Mortensen's riding remains excellent. Both actors ride big sorrel Quarter Horses with blaze faces and socks, in homage to John Wayne's horse preference: men do look great on such magnificent, fancy beasts.

Slow West (2015) and *The Power of the Dog* (2021)

Another western film in desperate need of horses with personality and plot is *Slow West* (2015), which seems to believe that featuring Michael Fassbender (1977–) on horseback is enough to propel a doomed journey. Fassbender rides well and looks fetching on horseback, as he does doing just about anything; however, the horses are mere props for the picaresque journey west that Silas (Fassbender) and Jay (Kodi Smit-McPhee) take in search of the latter's lost love.

Having had close relationships with so many horses in my life, I know only too well that they have personalities, sometimes terrible ones. Having a hunk on a horse simply isn't enough to enlist one's interest, though the handsome Fassbender looks great in the grit and grime of the old West. In the genre of hunks on horseback, Costner and Mortensen receive the merit badges, but the rest of the films noted forget that the hunk needs an equally hunky horse for the film to work.

Kodi Smit-McPhee (1996–) also stars in director Jane Campion's (1954–) 2021 pseudo-western *The Power of the Dog*, a powerful if perplexing film, though Smit-McPhee is equally compelling, rides well, and (finally) moves the plot forward. The horses are primarily secondary, except for one scene in which embittered Phil (Benedict Cumberbatch) take out his rage at his brother's new wife, the McPhee character's mother, on a horse, cursing at it, punching it in the face over and over, with the terrified horse backing away and Phil following, still cursing and hitting. The scene is so real that I wondered if New Zealand, where the movie was filmed, had any regulations or laws relating to the protection of animals performing in film. Though there isn't a specific statute for animals in film, there are strict penalties for animal abuse, involving significant prison time (three to five years) and fines up to $100,000 for individuals and up to $500,000 for corporate entities, and these are even more severe if the ill-treatment is found to be reckless disregard for the safety and health of the animal. The film's head horse and animal coordinator, Lizzie Lam, has no other credits for her work with animals, though she has crewed numerous TV shows and movies in the art department. One can only hope she managed to make this very disturbing scene without reckless disregard for the realistically terrified horse.

One other scene in *The Power of the Dog* stays in the horse lover's mind. Toward the film's surprising climax, a seismic shift in power on the ranch takes place, having to do with the aforementioned rage-filled Phil, who rules the ranch with an iron hand and caustic mouth. This comes at the hand of Peter (Smit-McPhee), whose eerie and quiet presence turns out to represent not weakness but a near-psychopathic strength and coldness. And for one scene, even the horses are aware that something has changed in the air. One horse looks out on this new world with concern bordering on alarm, its eyes wide, looking at nothing but knowing all. The other horses in the paddock mill about, and some beautiful shots of the sun on their backs and manes as they remain unusually restive tells us all we need to know about Phil's reign of terror. Something has changed, and the horses, sensitive to fear and insanity and newness, realize it. It is a strange interlude from all the psychological drama and makes us aware that even nature has been altered at this toxic home place. This film haunts you, just as the horses, the most empathic of animals, are at this moment haunted.

The Mask of Zorro (1998) and *The Legend of Zorro* (2005)

Another film featuring a hunk on horseback and a lighthearted approach is *The Mask of Zorro* (1998), starring hunky Antonio Banderas (1960–) as the inheritor of the Zorro mask, as the original Zorro, Don Diego de la Vega (Anthony Hopkins, 1937–), has grown too old for serious swashbuckling. But he sees something of promise in the young Alejandro Murrieta (Banderas) and trains him for the role of great swordsman, defender of the common man and Indigenous people against the Spanish oligarchy, and chameleon, able to pretend to be an aristocrat to infiltrate the Spanish dons. And, of course, to ride like nobody's business. Directed by Martin Campbell (1943–), known for making fun adventures, including those of James Bond and various superheroes, the film strikes a perfect tone: dramatic, romantic, and funny.

We are clued in to the nature of horses in this film when the younger Don Diego (Hopkins), as Zorro on an exploit against the urbane, corrupt governor of the California province, whistles once and his coal-black horse Tornado appears out of nowhere; Diego jumps on him and rides him back to their cave. They have a conversation about how both of them are getting too old for these adventures; the horse vocalizes and puts his head against Diego's chest. The delight of being in Bobby Lovgren–world, the best horse trainer in the business for creating horses who are characters and not just transportation, is palpable. The black horse wears gorgeous, silver-encrusted Spanish tack and is himself quite the hunk as he escapes from the governor's armed camp, riding across roofs, rearing.

Home from this latest adventure, Diego has little time for his beautiful wife and baby's warm welcome, for the evil governor Rafael shows up with soldiers to arrest Diego for his traitorous alter ego who defends the poor. In the ensuing melee, Diego's wife is shot, Diego is put into chains and arrested, and Rafael, who had been in love with Diego's wife, takes the baby, Elena, to raise as his own, vowing to leave Diego with nothing left of his life and throwing him into jail.

Fast-forward several years, and two bandit brothers, Joaquin Murrieta (Victor Rivers) and Alejandro Murrieta (Antonio Banderas), who had met Zorro as children, encounter, with their henchman Three-Finger Jack, Mexican soldiers led by an American cavalry officer, Captain Harry Love. Joaquin is captured and shoots himself, while Alejandro escapes.

This is where this adventure/comedy and real history intersect. Joaquin Murrieta (1829–1853) was a famous bandit in old California, a Mexican who came to California with his family, including siblings, during the gold rush. Instead of gold, Murrieta encountered thievery, cheating, and racism from both the whites and the Spanish dons, infuriating the previously honest, hardworking miner to become a renowned bandit, the Robin Hood of Mexico, who vowed to better the lives of downtrodden Mexicans in the California Territory. Murrieta was indeed shot dead by a California Ranger, Harrison Love, who had the corpse decapitated and kept the head, pickled, in a large jar of whiskey; he did the same, in a separate whiskey-filled jar, with the missing-fingered hand of Three-Finger Jack. These two horrible relics supposedly still exist in a contemporary collector's shop of horrors. Though there was no brother named Alejandro, the stories are remarkably similar; one old California historian insisted that Joaquin Murrieta was the inspiration for the heroic figure of Zorro.

Don Diego trains the coarse, undisciplined, vengeful Alejandro to become the next Zorro. He turns him into a matchless swordsman and athlete while inculcating in him that the people need Zorro to protect them from the power-hungry dons, and Alejandro does indeed turn into the inheritor of the persona of the Mexican Robin Hood. He even gets his own Tornado, a glistening, pure black Friesian stallion with a mischievous streak. The Friesian may be the most beautiful breed of horses, with its muscled body, keen head, wavy mane and tail, and feathering above all four hooves, and it is known for its beauty of movement and grace. Three Friesians and Bobby Lovgren's American Quarter Horse, Houdini, dyed from his original buckskin to black, played Tornado, though the main actor playing Tornado was named Casey, and he did most of the acting in the film. Houdini was known for his almost completely vertical rear, standing straight up and pawing the air vigorously, the perfect image for Zorro on horseback. Houdini was a son of the greatest Quarter Horse racing stallion, Dash for Cash, who was among the most handsome horses I've ever seen, so Houdini's good looks make perfect sense. In his natural state, he portrays the mount of Captain Love, who hunted down the Murrieta brothers and serves the corrupt California governor loyally. (Houdini was also used by James Cameron in stop-motion, computerized form in *Avatar*.) Banderas, already a creditable rider and athlete, became far better as filming continued, according to Lovgren, and especially enjoyed riding the spirited Casey.

When Alejandro first attempts to mount his own Tornado, the black horse does everything in his power to buck him off, smashing through walls and misbehaving in general. He is never the disciplined mount that Don Diego enjoyed in his Zorro heyday, vocalizing complaints about work to Alejandro, failing to respond to commands in English as he pretends to speak only Spanish, and being generally mischievous with Alejandro. I actually had a client bring me a huge Hanoverian, supposedly trained in dressage in Germany, who was impossible to ride and paid no attention to commands. I was supposed to "fix" him. I immediately thought that perhaps the horse didn't speak English and tried German on him, achieving only the same blank look in his clearly intelligent eyes. Then it occurred to me that the language of dressage is French, and I spoke to him in French. Voilà! He was a willing mount. When I'd chastise him for picking on his smaller paddock mates at mealtime, I'd say, "Vous êtes un tête du merde!" and he would bow his head, arch his neck, and paw the air with one front foot, apologizing.

Of course, Alejandro meets the equally swashbuckling Elena (giving the film a feminist slant), who believes herself to be the governor's daughter, and brings her together with her real father, Don Diego, while engaging in many fencing matches and eventually besting the corrupt governor and gaining freedom for the Indigenous people. There is also an homage to the movie *Spartacus*. When Don Diego is in jail, the governor's wardens come to question all the prisoners, demanding to know which one of them is Zorro. This scene turns into a twin of the rousing "I am Spartacus" scene in that movie, when every man claims to be Spartacus, protecting the real one's identity but also demonstrating their unity in ending their enslavement and in their courage.

But there is another, far more thrilling homage in the film. Remember Ben Johnson and Harry Carey Jr., performing Roman riding in *Rio Grande*? This impossible-looking stunt requires the horseman to stand on two horses, one foot on each, and the amazingly gifted horseman Johnson even takes a jump. Zorro, while chasing the governor's forces, is Roman riding on two of their horses for this stunt and even jumps over a tree limb in his path while continuing this spectacular stunt. Lovgren even features the crupper mount that John Ford insisted on. Bobby Lovgren duplicates what Ford required Johnson and Carey to do, the gymnastic mount, from the ground, over the horse's hip, by planting one's hands on the horse's croup and vaulting forward into the saddle. Banderas's stunt double, Tad Griffith, performs this stunt with ease, using a pair of his own mares, sisters, whom he'd worked together as long as he'd had them. It should be noted that doubling Banderas as Zorro was easily achieved, as Zorro is always masked, hatted, and dressed all in black.

I've avoided dealing with sequels, as they are usually anemic versions of the original, but the sequel to *The Mask of Zorro*, *The Legend of Zorro* (2005), also directed by Martin Campbell, demands attention because of another homage to John Ford and the enlarging of Tornado's antics, giving the horse even more to do. Bobby Lovgren once again trained the horses, and from the beginning, the film demonstrates his trademarks. Under the opening credits, one sees the straight-up rearing of Tornado, ridden by Zorro, and we are once again in Lovgrenland. When Alejandro, drunk, drops his whiskey bottle, Tornado picks it up and drinks from it; when Elena drops her pipe, the horse picks it up and smokes it. This sequel features an unnecessarily complicated and perplexing plot, full of secrets to be revealed, but the horse action scenes are truly captivating. Alejandro and the French count Armand take part in a duel/jousting match/polo match, ended when Elena loosens Alejandro's horse's girth so that his saddle slips and he falls off. Tornado, Zorro, and a rescued infant leap out of a fiery barn. Tornado flips a railroad switch with his front hooves to keep two trains from colliding. Zorro and Tornado leap from a high cliff onto a moving train, and they ride atop the train, crashing through the roof of a train car when presented with a tunnel before them, a motif Lovgren will repeat, even more thrillingly, in *The Lone Ranger*.

Lovgren can't resist paying homage, though, to one of the greatest stunts in movie history, Yakima Canutt's falling between a team of raging horses in *Stagecoach* (1939). Canutt's character, in Indian garb, is trampled, while the real Canutt is saved by his own trompe l'oeil, the creation of a special, enlarged coupling of the horses that remains invisible to the viewer. In *The Legend of Zorro*, Zorro falls between a team of horses, imitating Canutt, and positions himself perfectly between them to live to tell the tale. How Lovgren achieved this is unknown, though he clearly used fearless stuntmen and may have used Canutt's own enlarged coupling. Both of these films are boundlessly enhanced by horsemanship and thrilling stunts, a paean to Lovgren and his crew, who are willing to do the impossible.

The Assassination of Jesse James by the Coward Robert Ford (2007) and *The Long Riders* (1980)

Perhaps the most beautiful looking western ever made, *The Assassination of Jesse James by the Coward Robert Ford* (2007) features cinematographer Roger Deakins (think all of the Coen brothers' films) at his very best, working for a director, Andrew Dominik (1967–), in no hurry to get anywhere, starring our time's transcendent, ageless hunk, Brad Pitt. Like *No Country for Old Men*, this is a faithful and impressive adaptation of the novel by Ron Hansen, and keeps the novel's tragic, elegiac tone. Thinking about Brad Pitt on a horse seems an excellent idea; however, the movie's psychological approach to a Jesse James always on the edge of madness and violence somehow can't be made to include horses. The horse characters seem to have no feelings or personalities whatsoever, except for a single line from Brad Pitt to his horse after he shoots and kills a gang member whom he imagines to be a traitor (paranoia is part of the psychological profile of this Jesse) and the horse spooks. Jesse pats the horse's neck and says, "It's okay, sweetheart."

Another film that celebrates the beauty of horses without appreciating their emotional intelligence is *The Long Riders* (1980), directed by Walter Hill (1940–) and with cinematography by the masterful Ric Waite. This movie too is about the James Gang, and its brilliance resides in its casting. Gaggles of Keaches, Carradines, and Quaids play, respectively, Frank and Jesse James, the Youngers, and the Millers (specifically Stacy and James Keach; Robert, Keith, and David Carradine; and Dennis and Randy Quaid); the real-life sets of brothers provide an unparalleled level of authenticity to the casting. The film opens with a glorious slow-motion shot of all the gang members galloping their horses in tandem, but if you're watching for horse glory, that's about all you get. There is a moment when Jesse picks out his horse's hoof realistically and one superb stunt when gang members jump their horses through a storefront's glass window to escape a trap, but otherwise, *The Long Riders* disappoints in its usage of horses, another missed opportunity. As well, though the players try their best, they are clearly actors trying to ride rather than bandits riding. They bounce and move about in the saddle clumsily, demonstrating that riding lessons are no match for those few actors who are real riders, like Costner, Mortensen, and Banderas.

Wyatt Earp (1994) and *Tombstone* (1993)

As we began with Costner, so we end with Costner and a tale of two movies, both about Wyatt Earp. In 1993, Kevin Jarre (1954–2011) was set to direct the movie *Tombstone*, starring Kevin Costner. But Costner was unhappy with the script, which was essentially an ensemble piece. The star wanted the script rewritten to focus on his character alone (looks like a case of inflated ego and narcissism brought on by the success and Oscar wins for 1990's *Dances with Wolves*), but Jarre believed in his script and refused. Costner quit the film, leaving Jarre and the script on the proverbial studio shelf. Meanwhile, Costner began putting together his own Wyatt Earp film, focusing intently on Earp himself and getting Lawrence Kasdan (*Silverado*, *The Big Chill*) to write a script with Dan Gordon that would be a star turn for the seemingly self-important and self-serious actor. Just because a guy can ride doesn't make him a wonderful person.

Tombstone (1993) did get made, though without Jarre as director; instead, George Cosmatos (1941–2005), a journeyman with *Leviathan* and other unremarkable films to his credit, was brought in to direct, and Kurt Russell was hired to portray Wyatt Earp. The ensemble cast included charismatic actors like Powers Boothe, Michael Biehn (he of the craziest eyes in film), Sam Elliot, and Bill Paxton, though Val Kilmer, as Doc Holliday, was as big a scene-stealer as any child star or adorable animal. Kilmer lost thirty pounds to play the tubercular gambler and gunslinger and gives a performance laced with humor, irony, and a self-awareness of how much fun playing Holliday can be.

The film opens with a shot of a group of men on horseback, each horse a glorious creature galloping across the screen, and throughout, the film demonstrates a love of and appreciation for horses. Early on, Earp comes to the aid of a horse that is being savagely beaten because it won't get off a train car, and horse lovers are sucked in. A plus is that both Russell and Kilmer ride like cowboys rather than actors, unmoving in the saddle. Kilmer's eponymous documentary, *Val* (2021), shows him riding on his six-thousand-acre ranch in New Mexico, so he is the real deal.

The best horse scene occurs when Wyatt meets, by chance, the actress Josie Marcus (Dana Delaney); he, on his plain dark bay stallion, is immediately smitten with her, on her white mare. The horses arch their necks, breathe into each other's noses, and seem instantly smitten, just as Wyatt is with his first glimpse of Josie. Wyatt suggests that Josie's mare is in heat and that they would be better off separating, but Josie, ever the adventuress, suggests that they gallop the interest in mating out of them and sets off running, with Wyatt following. The behavior of the horses is realistic, an indication of "teasing" to see if a mare is willing to accept a stallion, and the scene uses the horses as a metaphor for the attraction between Wyatt and Josie.

Though no head horse trainer is credited for *Tombstone*, an army of stuntmen, buckaroos, and wranglers coordinated the horse work, and there are a couple of pretty dazzling stunts. Wyatt, in pursuit of bad men, jumps his horse through a shop window, taking a shortcut to capture them. And in the infamous vengeful posse pursuit of the Clanton Gang after the murder of Morgan Earp, Wyatt rides, at a full gallop, off the side of his horse, peeking around the front of the horse to fire at the bad guys, in stellar stunt work. After killing nearly the lot of the Clantons, Wyatt and Holliday shake hands on galloping horses, saluting a job well done by both.

The Costner/Kasdan *Wyatt Earp* was released in 1994 and runs just over three hours, though it feels like three years. We are forced to endure about an hour of Earp's childhood and family and watch as his saccharine first marriage to a longtime sweetheart ends in tragedy, turning Earp dark, self-destructive, and mean. Though this is true to history—Earp was dark and mean and coldhearted throughout his life and was as much a criminal as a lawman, having a checkered past filled with arrests for pimping and thieving and fixing prize fights. In the film, many other characters call Earp "coldhearted," and he does seem to be; however, Costner's acting gives us little clue as to what is going on inside Earp's head, as he just seems limp and weak and lacking in empathy. Costner's light, uninflected voice doesn't help, and his acting seems lost, just as his character is. Three hours of a brooding Earp/Costner is two hours too many, and one longs for the end of the film.

And the horses! They are missing in action. Costner's riding ability was highlighted in both *Silverado* and *Dances with Wolves*, but in this endless, glum, solemn, wandering, would-be epic, Costner doesn't ride. This self-serious Wyatt has little to do but brood and stare off into the distance when he could be riding hands-free. It's as if Costner wanted to carry this film as an actor, not as a talented rider, demonstrating his lack of understanding of his ability and what made him attractive in previous films. Though the gifted Rusty Hendrickson is the head wrangler, he had little to do in this inflated biopic. *Wyatt Earp* was a box office flop, losing money, while *Tombstone* doubled its $25 million budget at the box office. Wyatt Earp got justice finally, and we got Val Kilmer as Doc Holliday saying, "I'm your huckleberry."

The shame in the troubled *Wyatt Earp* is that if Costner wanted to go dark and dismantle the myth of Wyatt Earp, why didn't he go all the way? Earp was a scoundrel; his beloved Josie was, in real life, a prostitute and a shrew; and his lauded friendship with Doc Holliday ended when Doc accused him of "turning into a Jew boy" because Josie placed a mezuzah at their front door and Wyatt would touch it when entering. But Costner had to be heroic and so went only superficially dark, begetting this endless, boring, skin-deep movie and successfully stanching all of Lawrence Kasdan's sense of fun. I lived in Las Vegas, New Mexico, in 1993 and witnessed some of the filming of *Wyatt Earp*, and it was not a fun set. (I'd been on many other movie sets when I was a journalist and believe that lighthearted sets turn out the better films.) Grim work, being Wyatt Earp, if you're Kevin Costner, and grimmer work: attempting to make it through this film.

The real Wyatt Earp (1848–1929) has one item in his favor. Late in life, he lived in Southern California and liked to go out drinking with his friends, cowboy actors William S. Hart and Tom Mix. Through them he met a fledgling film director, to whom he told stories of the old West. That director was John Ford, who would later make his own Wyatt Earp film, *My Darling Clementine* (1946), a great western starring Henry Fonda as Earp and Victor Mature as Doc Holliday; its one downfall is that it lacks horse charisma, like most Ford films that didn't include Ben Johnson or John Wayne.

9

Horse Whisperers

Everyone who loves horses has had an ego-on-the-loose moment when she's thought, "I'm a horse whisperer," immediately after a moment of perfect understanding between human and horse that defies logic. If this moment happens to you, you need to whack yourself in the head with a cast-iron skillet and move on because having this thought guarantees that you are not a horse whisperer. Not that there aren't such beings, but the true horse whisperer is free of ego and doesn't think of himself much at all—at least in the movies. (Consider the case of famous trainer Monty Roberts—in reality, a tremendous ego but able to talk to horses. Why they listen to him is a mystery to me. But his special trick is taking an untrained horse and, within a few minutes, making him rideable.) For the uninitiated, a horse whisperer is someone with an ability to commune and communicate with horses in a transcendental way, in a way that goes beyond any known language or discipline. It's a fabulous concept, especially for the movies. Communion between man and horse is a cinematic wonder, and some truly memorable horses exist in movies about horse whisperers. There are such memorable horses in *The Horse Whisperer* and in the documentary *Buck*, and there should have been in the dreadful film adaptation of *All the Pretty Horses*.

The Horse Whisperer (1998)

The Horse Whisperer (1998) holds the distinction of appearing in two separate categories, because it bestrides the narrow world of horse films like a colossus, existing in the "girls who love horses" and "horse whisperers" fields simultaneously. This doesn't mean it's such a great film—it is long and, in some places, tediously draggy. But it does boast an all-time great movie horse—Pilgrim.

Pilgrim is the beloved of Grace (Scarlett Johansson), and both are injured in what may be the most horrific accident ever portrayed in horse films: Two girls out for a bucolic dawn ride in a snowy countryside encounter an icy hill and a careening semitruck. One girl and her horse perish, and the other girl and her horse are injured almost unto death. Pilgrim, a handsome bay with a star, purchased in Kentucky for his jumping ability, rears up at the approaching truck, attempting to protect his beloved mistress, and suffers mysterious, supposedly life-threatening injuries because of this. Forever joined in love and tragedy, Grace loses part of her leg and her positive attitude on life, becoming a sour teenager because of the accident, and Pilgrim is battered beyond recognition and also loses his docile, petlike nature, turning into an angry, evil, Frankenstein's monster of a horse, cobbled together, it would appear, from various pieces of decaying horse flesh. Both horse and girl need to be reminded of love and hope, and who better to do that than Robert Redford (1936–), who also directed?

Four different horses play Pilgrim in the film, though Redford eschewed animatronic horses and computer-generated imagery, and all of the horse work is "real," just as he is a real horseman and horse lover. Hightower, a Quarter Horse, was the trained fighting horse who could be called off at a moment's notice, lucky for Redford. Cash and Maverick did some of the fighting scenes as well, though trainer Rex Peterson, who studied with legends Tom Dorrance and Ray Hunter, found them less amiable and willing to forget their anger. The fourth horse star is Buck Brannaman's own horse, Pet,

The Horse Whisperer, 1998. Robert Redford soothes the crazed Pilgrim. Directed by Robert Redford. (Buena Vista/Photofest. ©Buena Vista.)

who stood in for the others when a trick couldn't be achieved by Peterson and his horses.

The question whether to put Pilgrim down after the accident seems sincere, if mysterious. In my experience, vets want to save horses, not kill them, and a horse with all four legs intact and no visible, potentially fatal injuries is a good subject for veterinary salvation. But the vet insists he is now scarred beyond redemption. How she can assume psychological scarring demanding euthanasia at the scene of the accident strains belief, but she keeps insisting it to be necessary—a manufactured part of the soapy drama and another instance of veterinary negligence so common in horse movies anxious for drama instead of realism.

The horsemanship in *The Horse Whisperer* is accurate and compelling, with Tom (Redford) using humane and compassionate methods without any cruelty to return the horse to useful sanity. He uses a combination of Monty Roberts's and Buck Brannaman's techniques in the round pen with Pilgrim and outlasts the escaped horse in a staring contest while squatting in a paddock, a technique I have used with mares who do not want to get caught for vets or farriers. If you make yourself very small, horses' natural curiosity will draw them to you. There is even an opinion offered on foal imprinting, a methodology that found vast acceptance about twenty or thirty years ago, in which a human is supposed to force her attentions on a newborn foal, getting it used to being touched all over and even introducing it to such things as clippers, in those important early hours when the mare's own intimate bond with her baby is being formed. The movie doesn't believe in imprinting, and I don't either. Letting the day-old foal come to you, again out of innate curiosity, makes the foal the initiator of your friendship, a far better way to build trust with a baby.

The Horse Whisperer is in love with horses' eyes, primarily those of the great Pilgrim. If there are better close-ups than these of horses' eyes, I'd like to see them. The luminous soul and reflection of oneself in a horse's eyes are both moving and touching. Pilgrim's eyes contain all the pain and love in this movie and seem to demand compassion. "Understand my pain," they seem to be saying. Tom (Redford) does. The portrayal of the total patience and calm one needs to work with difficult horses, if not all horses, is accurate and moving, and Tom cures both Pilgrim and Grace with his profound humanity. I truly believe that people who love animals, and horses in particular, become more human and humane through their attempts to comprehend the needs of other species.

I'm almost willing to forgive the film its equine lapses. For example, when Kristin Scott Thomas sets off to drive Pilgrim from New York City to Montana for psychotherapy—a very lengthy trip for even the most seasoned horse hauler—she responds to a naysayer by offering that the horse will be sedated. If there's a sedation that lasts for four or five days without being repeated, I'd love to know about it, as I have hauled cantankerous horses all over this earth. Pilgrim has developed a murderous rage—how do they get water and food to him in the trailer without losing fingers or hands? Does he simply stand in the trailer for days? If so, that won't improve his mien. And who gets him off the trailer and into a small corral at a motel for Tom's perusal and, later, loaded again and rereleased at Tom's ranch? As someone who's loaded and unloaded intransigent, even murderous, horses, I know this is a risky endeavor, not meant for the editor of a self-consciously cool magazine and her physically and emotionally damaged daughter.

Pilgrim makes you forget all about this. He's scarred and raw, with fire in his eyes, mad at the world that harmed him. He's all passion and flame, anger igniting him into rearing and pawing in nearly every early scene. A piratical horse, with that scarred, skinless face and multiple wounds, he is the wild heart of this movie, making all the human stars look pallid and small-spirited. Pilgrim's rage knows no bounds. The four horses who play him are wonderful actors, on a level with Joe Pesci in *Goodfellas* (1990) in terms of ability to demonstrate maniacal anger. There exists, in the film, the very true idea that horses force us to open our hearts to them in compassion and empathy if we are even semi-human—a very good thing—and the theme of redemption for Grace and Pilgrim is moving because of this reality.

Buck (2011)

In the wonderful documentary *Buck* (2011), directed by Cindy Meehl (1957–) about real-life horse whisperer Buck Brannaman (1962–), there is a horse that makes Pilgrim look like an advertisement for the benefits of anger management. There isn't anyone who has seen this film who can forget Kelly, the killer stallion, owned by an utterly clueless woman who keeps eighteen wild stallions. Buck looks at her with the pity reserved for the truly touched in the head. Kelly, a handsome palomino Quarter Horse type with white on his face, is the most terrifying horse ever seen in film, the reincarnation of Rex the Devil Horse without any of his talents, only his murderous personality.

Brannaman holds the distinction of having been a consultant (equine technical adviser) on *The Horse Whisperer*, after which he told Redford, "If this film acting thing doesn't work out for you, you might just have a future as a cowboy." When none of the film's wranglers could get the horse playing Pilgrim to perform a specific set of actions for a scene—tapping his foot on a mark and then putting his head against Scarlett Johansson's chest in a perfect horse hug, indicating the beginning of his healing—Brannaman got his horse to do the scene in twenty minutes, and his horse, made up so that he resembled the maimed horse, then performed as stunt double for Pilgrim. Brannaman's quiet, patient mien makes him able to transform and teach both equine and human, and he informs the character of Tom with his goodness.

In the documentary, Kelly comes to one of Buck's clinics; his pathetic owner hopes that the famous horse whisperer can turn this monster into a teddy bear. Kelly was brain damaged at birth, and all he knows how to express is rage. In contrast to the fictional Pilgrim, who had his life altered by an accident, the real Kelly is evil from birth, without hope of return to any world of sanity and kindness. He has the evil shining beauty of an equine Lucifer and has been allowed to grow up wild and unneutered. Before Buck comprehends the profundity of Kelly's ineradicable evil, he gets one of his helpers to mount the horse while the horse is hobbled, and it doesn't go all that badly. First attempts of anything with horses are frequently like this—the horses are too surprised to act out. But on the second attempt, without hobbles, Kelly understands that he has his chance, and he just about bites the poor cowboy's face off in an obvious attempted murder. The man is lucky to exit the corral alive, and even so, he is covered in blood and needs a hasty trip to the emergency room.

When the unflappable Buck works with Kelly in a tiny corral, we fear for Buck—like Superman facing Lex Luther, Batman squaring off against Bane, or Holyfield fighting Tyson, anything can happen. Kelly is nature unleashed in evil fury—what chance can good stand against such a force? Kelly is the antithesis of everything the horse is and should be—as a species, horses are cooperative, loving, and gentle, and usually only fear inspires them to harm their humans (though, just as there are evil humans, evil horses do exist, and I have known some). Kelly is different—he aspires to harm and destruction, as any supervillain does. When Buck, using his signature flags on sticks, gets Kelly loaded into the crazy woman's trailer, his relief is palpable. I held my breath, waiting for something ghastly to happen to Buck, until Kelly was on that trailer and heading off, possibly to euthanasia. In a postscript, Buck has one last conversation with Kelly's owner, hugs her, and tells her she can't risk her life with this horse, who would not hesitate to kill her.

One can't help thinking that Buck's experience with Kelly informed some of his work on *The Horse Whisperer*, because postaccident Pilgrim resembles Kelly in his dark fury at the world that has maimed him. In *The Horse Whisperer*, Tom tells Grace's mother, Annie, during their first phone call that he doesn't help people with horse problems. He helps horses with people problems. This line is taken directly from Buck's clinics and draws attention to how fully Buck has informed the character of Tom. Tom wears Buck's signature silver bracelet in the film, carries his coiled rope at his thigh like Buck, and the photo in Tom's family's house of Tom as a small boy in an enormous cowboy hat is really a photo of the young Buck. That Tom is presented with Pilgrim, who resembles Kelly but for whom salvation is possible, underscores the Buck/Tom twinning. Buck also doubles for Redford in some scenes, uncredited. In the documentary *Buck*, Redford relates how much a part of the film's story and the filming Brannaman became, and the evidence supports this. Brannaman is that rare creature in film, the truly good man who isn't sappy or melodramatic. Just the opposite, in fact: he is matter-of-fact to his students and transforms them through his genuine warmth and humanity, making him both a horse and human whisperer. *Buck* must be seen by all horse lovers. Like many of the horses he whispers to, Buck himself was terribly abused as a child by an evil stage father, so the compassion he brings to students and horses alike is based on his own scarring. Much like Pilgrim, he has been redeemed in an opposite plot twist: man saved by horses rather than horses saved by man.

All the Pretty Horses (2000)

At the opposite end of the horse spectrum is the film *All the Pretty Horses* (2000). It's a terrible film adaptation of a great book (published in 1992), the latter set firmly in Cormac McCarthy–world in which no good deed goes unpunished and love is doomed from the start, but it is full of great horse characters, in particular the huge blood bay that the urchin Jimmy Blevins rides. Those who are aficionados of horse history and breeding cannot help but be fascinated by McCarthy's encyclopedic horse knowledge, which gives the book a foundation in the real world. Where Jimmy Blevins got (stole?) such a horse isn't revealed, but both of the main characters, John Grady Cole and his best friend, Lacy Rawlins, opine, in their monosyllabic fashion, about the horse numerous times: "That's one hell of a horse." As someone who loves to inhabit Cormac McCarthy–world, I longed to see the Blevins horse, but in the film version, he is just a horse rather than a horse god. There should be many other stellar horses here—John Grady's saddle horse Redbo, Alejandra's beautiful black Arabian, the Thoroughbred stallion Alejandra's father imports to improve his remuda and whom John rides with sexual abandon in the book, and Rawlins's horse Junior. But no horse is granted the character of Pilgrim or Kelly, and John Grady Cole's mystical ability with horses disappears into a sappy love story that could just as easily be horse-free.

The novel features a set piece in which John Grady Cole (Matt Damon) sets out to break sixteen wild horses in a day—an impossible feat. He has his partner Lacy helping him, but no mortal can achieve this. In the book, though, John Grady Cole isn't exactly a mortal. His gift for horsemanship extends beyond mere skill, into the realm of the divine, the magical, the transcendental, and McCarthy loves to write about the way in which the boy, frequently called the Breaker, communicates with wild horses, calming them and getting them to do his bidding. The horses, crazy-eyed and seething, are wonderful in their angry confusion. The scene turns into a sort of carnival attraction, with local families coming out to watch the crazy gringos in their impossible quest. Lacy helps, but John Grady Cole's mystical abilities to commune with even the wildest horses creates the success of this venture. A world without horses is impossible for Cole. He is the one pure soul in the book (reminiscent of Buck Brannaman), the admirer of all that is ardent and wild and filled with passion, and because of this certainly doomed. In the book, Cole uses methods of kindness, compassion, and understanding to sooth the wild horses and communicate with them on a wavelength unknown to other men.

The film trivializes and brutalizes this central scene from the book, the scene that gives Cole his bona fides as the Sir Lancelot of this arid, dehumanizing landscape. It's just a couple of boys breaking horses—no big deal. Cole is no better or worse at it than Lacy Rawlins. They are abrupt and mean in their approach, throwing saddles on the hobbled horses and getting bucked off for their efforts, until the exhausted animals give up. And the quixotic aspect of much of the book, the pursuit of the impossible by the implausible, can't exist in the film. In the book, Cole is sixteen, Rawlins seventeen, and Alejandra seventeen. The two boys riding their horses into Mexico seem ridiculous when it's Matt Damon (1970–), clearly nearing thirty, leading the way, and his doomed love for Alejandra, played by a midtwenties Penelope Cruz (1974–), just seems ill-conceived and silly. Both are old enough to know better. Both are beyond an age of innocence, which McCarthy chose to portray with his teenaged characters in the book, a western Romeo and Juliet. Just as Shakespeare knew that Romeo and Juliet had to be adolescents or their love would appear mere foolishness, so too does McCarthy give us teenagers propelled into an emotional hurricane they are ill equipped to comprehend or even live through. The film simply doesn't get this and doesn't connect Cole's passion for horses with his love for Alejandra. Cole is all in and can't love halfway—his intensity is as young as his years, but it makes for a charming hero. With Cole so diminished, turned into a love-crazed adult idiot, so too does his love of horses become smaller and sillier, and as a result, the horses in the movie become mere background instead of admired characters.

Billy Bob Thornton (1955–) directed this botched film, with a screenplay by Ted Tally, who wrote the beautifully scripted adaptation of *The Silence of the Lambs* (1991), turning it into a multilayered, rich charactered film, so I hesitate to lay the blame for this film on him. Mike Nichols was initially slated to direct, and I can't help but think what a different, and better, film this might have been, though turning my favorite novel into a movie would have been a tough task for anyone. Part of the allure of the book for horse lovers is McCarthy's encyclopedic knowledge of horses, their personalities, breeding, and pedigrees. All of his horse wisdom rings true and is portrayed with love through the eyes of John Grady Cole. The film, cold and lacking in genuine horse knowledge, as well as downright ignorant in its portrayal of first love, is a failure that must be laid at the feet of Thornton. His directorial career was stymied after the box office failure of *All the Pretty Horses*, and though he received an Oscar nomination for the screenplay of his film *Sling Blade* (1996), hardly known for its sensitivity and depth, he has not made another film that has equaled its singular success. He was simply the wrong man for the big job that *All the Pretty Horses* presented. How I wish someone with horse knowledge and horse love had instead directed this film, turning it into a spectacular, fully imagined world. Even Kevin Costner would have done a better job, as he clearly has profound feeling for the world of the horse.

10

Ridley Scott and Horses

I will see any Ridley Scott movie if there are horses in it, no matter the reviews (and the reviews for *Kingdom of Heaven* and *Exodus* were toxic), because no one understands as well as Scott how thrilling horses can be. Scott understands that one hundred horses are infinitely more thrilling than ten, and a thousand horses—off the Richter scale. What Scott loves and understands is the Horse, rather than any single horse. Scott's ability to stage huge battle scenes, as in *Kingdom of Heaven* and *Gladiator*, or the movement of masses of humans on horses, as in *Exodus: Gods and Kings*, is unequaled.

Strangely, Scott is best known for his science fiction, including *Blade Runner*, *Alien*, *Prometheus*, and *The Martian*. But there are no horses in outer space. Still, what Scott loves is the painstaking creation of a milieu, making it completely believable because of attention to detail, and this attention graces both his science fiction (whole civilizations were created for *Prometheus*) and his historical genre. He loves to dress his horses in the costume of the historical age of the film. Note the chariots and finery of ancient Rome on display on horses from *Gladiator*, the biblical costumery of *Exodus* (though one can't help but wonder if he reused some of his *Gladiator* horse clothing here—more great chariots, for example), and the wondrous Crusades–era garb for horses in *Kingdom of Heaven* and *Robin Hood*.

Ridley Scott was born on November 30, 1937, in Northumberland, part of the northwestern area of England that is grimy and industrialized, not known for its wealth of horses. He is determinedly closemouthed about his childhood, though we know his father was a brigadier general who worked with Churchill and moved the family to Germany after the war because of his posting. Scott is one of those military brats who attended double-digit schools, but his father's military discipline made a mark on this sensitive, artistic child, as did his mother's strength of character. Any horse lover, however, recognizes a kindred spirit in Scott, and he began drawing remarkably lifelike horses at age six. Where did this Geordie kid get acquainted with horses? The answer is simple: the movies.

"My first love . . . is Westerns," Scott said in an interview. "I was obsessed with cowboys and Indians when I was a kid. And I was a very keen horseman. I learned to ride when I was nine." He also noted, referring to western movies, "I was absolutely embedded in the notion of being in that world." The introverted, artistic kid went to the movies every chance he got. It's likely that his family moving to Germany afforded him the opportunity to ride, as at nine he was living there, probably even more introverted because of language barriers and being uprooted. But as every horse lover knows, horses cure loneliness and depression. As Churchill is rumored to have said, "There is nothing so good for the inside of a man as the outside of a horse."

The stunning visuals Scott's movies are known for come from his artistic aptitude, and seven years of art school, including a graduate degree from the prestigious Royal School of Art in London, where his discovery of a movie camera in a long-forgotten closet launched him into his life's work. Scott has long desired to direct a western and spent years trying to develop Cormac McCarthy's epic novel *Blood Meridian* into a film, but even he, creator of the chest-bursting alien, was daunted by the violence in the work as well as its huge canvas—a shame, as it seems ideal for the overpopulated Scott frame. As he has said, "What I do best is universes."

Kingdom of Heaven (2005) and *Robin Hood* (2010)

Kingdom of Heaven (2005) takes place during the Crusades, and the frames are filled with animals—horses, camels, dogs, rodents, all of whom Scott clearly loves. Early on, though, one realizes a reason why Scott's horses are so fascinating. They are intelligent, emotionally complex beings, with awareness of and concern for the action going on around them. Tethered horses turn their heads back to watch the first battle, swords clanking, between Godfrey (Liam Neeson) and his men and the village sheriff and his men. A horse frightened by a clanging sword fight throws his rider in panic.

These horses aren't just vehicles for the actors; they respond emotionally to the heated action, as anyone who has been around horses knows they would do. The only off note I saw was the ease with which the cloaked men rode horses. Horses, a prey species, react badly to huge shadows over them that might be saber-toothed tigers or pterodactyls jumping them. I saw this firsthand when I put a citified friend on my most calm and bomb-proof horse to ride, and she made the mistake of trying to remove her jacket while in the saddle. The horse, named Sofa for her ease of riding, saw the black shadow behind her and freaked, running off with my poor friend still entangled in her jacket. Just getting the horses in the film to allow such garbed riders is a great training trick.

There is one memorable scene that defines the horses in *Kingdom of Heaven*: they fill the screen, pictured from the neck down, in a racehorse stagger as if coming out of a starting gate, their legs pumping in synchronicity, their muscles rippling, as they ride into battle (rumor has it that over two hundred horses appeared in *Kingdom of Heaven*). Scott switches to a slightly slowed motion, so that the details of the horses' extended legs and bulging muscles can be appreciated fully in this thrilling charge into battle. Only a horse lover could have filmed such a scene. Scott understands their power and grandeur better than any other director. Here, as in many westerns, horses are to be adored rather than used as cowboy-mobiles. Scott's use of slightly slowed motion, barely noticeable, heightens both the realism and the grandeur of horses in motion.

In another beautiful scene, Sybilla (Eva Green) appears at Balian's (Orlando Bloom) home to meet him, and she is aboard a glorious white Arabian, dressed to the teeth, around whose legs swirls a molten herd of greyhounds, like waves lapping at the Arab's hooves. This has to be one of the best entrances ever in the movies. Of course, Balian falls for her, having witnessed this. How could he not?

Another important element that Scott will use again is the exchange of a horse to immortalize friendship and respect between men. After a sheikh claims that the horse Balian rides is his because it is on his land, a fight ensues between Balian and the sheikh. The sheikh dies during the conflict, and the sheikh's henchman, whom Balian believes to be his servant, is given the handsome black horse (the oft-used George, stuntman and trainer Steve Dent's trusty trick horse) by Balian in sorrow that the sheikh's death has been caused. At the end, when the Saracens have conquered Jerusalem and are allowing Balian and his people to flee, the man, who is actually nobility, returns the lost horse to Balian, out of respect for his courage and compassion. Balian, a blacksmith at the movie's opening, has become ennobled both by his long-lost father, Godfrey, who is a baron, and by his own goodness of heart and courage. The beautiful horse is a fitting reward for such a man.

Scott also clearly values horsemanship, and Bloom rides like he was born in the saddle, as do all of the actors. Scott's regular crew of trainers and stuntmen, including the aforementioned Steve Dent and Peter White, clearly understand the director's love of the horse, and desire for man to coexist beautifully and realistically with horses. The horses in *Kingdom of Heaven* are among the most wonderful ever filmed. The film ends with the arrival of Richard the Lionheart, sacking Europe on his way to attempt the retaking of Jerusalem and looking for the valiant knight Balian, of whom he has heard. But Balian, having been through hell on the Crusades, has no further appetite for slaughter and tells the rider, "I am the blacksmith." To which Richard replies, "I am the king of England." Scott utilizes a huge list of stuntmen, wranglers, blacksmiths, and armorers for his horses, but it is Joel Proust who is given credit as horse master even though he usually works as an additional crew or stuntman. Here, he does a magnificent job, managing horses and stuntmen in both Spain and Morocco.

It is at this point that Scott's 2010 film *Robin Hood* begins, with Richard sacking Europe again on his way home from a failed Crusade, riding an exquisite, hot-tempered white horse. But this time, our hero is Robin Longstride (Russell Crowe), a lowly archer in Richard's army, fed up with the horrors of the Crusades much as Balian was. The landscape is filled with gorgeous hunks of horseflesh bedecked in medieval garb, and this time, the horses express their sentience by vocalizing in various ways indicating emotion: a whinny for fear, a snort for wanting to get started, a low growl for danger. Richard's white horse is clothed in such finery that he is clearly the horse fit for a king, making Richard as apparent to enemies as if he had a target on his forehead. With a short, masculine neck and a fine head, the horse is a stunner, though Richard, riding him for the assault on a castle, receives the inevitable arrow through the neck (shot by a cook serving soup to soldiers!), and the horse runs free. As in *Kingdom of Heaven*, Scott's egalitarian nature and distaste for the English caste system becomes evident.

Here Scott uses a similar trope to the one he used in *Kingdom of Heaven*, with a horse ennobling a commoner. Richard's white steed, found in the forest by coarse commoner Robin Longstride, is captured and ridden by Robin, in the clothing of the ambushed murdered knight Robert Loxley. Like Balian, Robin is ennobled by the horse and the knight's garb and carries out his promise to the dying Loxley to take Loxley's father's sword back to his father, a baron in Nottingham. The elder Loxley hatches a plan to have Robin pose as his son returned from the Crusades so that he still has an heir to his property; part of this bit of theater is that Robin must appear to be the husband of Marion, Robert's wife (played by Cate Blanchett). And yet he will become worthy of all of this, as he becomes the legendary Robin Hood and takes on the lying, dissolute, new king, John. The ownership of the king's horse confers aristocracy, and as in *Kingdom of Heaven*, a man's inner qualities (plus a fitting horse) are what make a true knight.

Scott loves choreographing scenes with scores of horses riding into battle, and his *Robin Hood* has these requisite shots, though they can't equal the scope of some of his other films. Still, the horse lover can't help but be pleased with *Robin Hood*, in which a lordly horse ennobles a commoner. Scott's historical adventures are pure horse heaven. Crowe, short and stout as his horse, rides credibly, and demonstrates an innate connection with the king's horse, who is as brave as his original owner was cowardly and dissolute. As in *Kingdom of Heaven*, Scott employs half of Hollywood and the United Kingdom to make *Robin Hood* compelling, with a list of stuntmen as long as that in the previous film, plus a horse trainer, Ricardo Cruz Jr.; a horse department led by Hana Bluchova; and a horse master, Peter White, who saw their horses safely through rugged Wales and much of England. In his attempts at universe creation, Scott becomes a one-man employment trend with his use of costumers, armorers, digital effects workers, and anyone who will contribute to the absolute verisimilitude of his films.

Gladiator (2000)

Of course, what is arguably Ridley Scott's best (and certainly most awarded) film, *Gladiator*, also has great horses in it. *Gladiator* (2000) was nominated for twelve Oscars, and won five, including Best Picture and Best Actor for Russell Crowe, though Ridley Scott lost Best Director to Stephen Soderburgh for his film *Traffic*, in one of the great enigmas of the Academy Awards. Crowe became a sort of a muse for Scott, appearing in *Robin Hood*, *A Good Year* (2006), *American Gangster* (2007), and, of course, *Gladiator*.

Gladiator predates *Kingdom of Heaven* by five years, and it's not surprising that some of the wonderful horse sequences, with horses lined up to go into battle, prefigure the best sequences in *Kingdom of Heaven*. As well, Scott dresses his horses up in great gear in *Gladiator* (the film's resident armorer was certainly kept busy), and Maximus (Crowe) rides Scott's signature white steed, a sign of heroism, grandeur, and nobility in the Scott pantheon. Animals once again inhabit many frames of the film, such as Maximus's poignant interaction with his dog before an early battle. The film also features camels, an elephant, a hyena, giraffes, lions, and a white pony being trained by Maximus's son right before he is killed.

Observe Maximus aboard his fearless white horse in the ensuing battle scene, riding as if part of the animal. Crowe doesn't have the cowboy body type that Kevin Costner has; instead, he's squat and muscular and has been paired with an equally muscular, short-necked, fiery-eyed horse that is clearly his heroic equal. Scott has noted that this film was inspired by *Spartacus* (1960) and *Ben-Hur* (1959), and the chariot scenes in the Colosseum are magnificent, with Scott, much like Yakima Canutt in the emblematic chariot scene in *Ben-Hur*, favoring teams of white horses and black horses that stand out against the dirt and grime of the Colosseum and the filthy rabble demanding the kill.

Gladiator offers one of the most dramatic openings in film, with the Roman military, led by Maximus and the emperor Marcus Aurelius, battling barbarians in Germania. Maximus rides his white steed into battle, along with the usual Scott hordes of horses, men, and brutality (as well as Maximus's war dog, a Neapolitan mastiff), and Scott's filming make man and horse exquisite together. Horses vocalize, rear, fall, trounce on downed men, and demonstrate in every way that they are every bit as sentient as the men on them, if not more so. *Gladiator* has been criticized for a lack of historical accuracy by classical scholars, but a specific element of the horse detailing is significant. The Roman soldiers ride saddles with stirrups. In reality, Roman soldiers rode saddles with two horns (front and back) and no stirrups, but the danger of such a historical choice made it unwise. As usual, Scott stalwart Steve Dent managed the horses and did stunts, demonstrating his skill and eighty-year family history in moviemaking with horses. From the opening scene of the barbarian battle, *Gladiator* is nothing less than true spectacle, and, as with Scott's other historical epics, demonstrates Scott's attention to detail and love of the overpopulated frame, so full of horses, men, other animals, and detail that the era created is lush with life and utterly believable.

It's interesting to note that the plot arc of *Gladiator* is the converse of the plot arcs of *Kingdom of Heaven* and *Robin Hood*, in each of which a commoner is ennobled both by a glorious horse and by personal rectitude. Maximus begins the movie as a celebrated general and person of so much importance in the empire that Caesar Marcus Aurelius anoints him to be his successor, before his evil son Commodus decides on an alternate, murderous plan. Captured by slavers, the important general is enslaved, trained to be a gladiator in the Roman Colosseum, and forced to fight to the death again and again. But still, his integrity and desire to survive ennoble him and make him a favorite of the rabble watching the games. Scott's concern with class and caste is once more obvious in this historical epic, as obvious as his love of the horse.

Exodus: Gods and Kings (2014) and *The Last Duel* (2021)

Exodus: Gods and Kings (2014), an odd biblical tale from atheist Scott, scrambles the same classist themes as *Gladiator*, *Kingdom of Heaven*, and *Robin Hood*. The character of Moses (Christian Bale) zigzags more than any of Scott's other main characters, as his enslaved Hebrew parents seek to save his life by putting him in a basket and sending him down a river, where he is found by an Egyptian princess and raised as her own. Moses becomes the trusted confidant of future pharaoh Ramses, the favorite of Ramses's father (much like Maximus in *Gladiator* is favored over Marcus Aurelius's own son Commodus), and a renowned general who saves Ramses's life in one of the many thrilling chariot battle scenes. Then, it is discovered Moses is actually

Hebrew, and he is sent into exile and experiences an assassination attempt as he is better off dead for the Egyptian rulers, who would rather not admit their error in raising a Hebrew child. After years of life as a simple shepherd, Moses encounters God, in the person of a rather petulant, capricious child who tells Moses he must free his people from slavery, and Moses is once again ennobled by this quest, at which he succeeds.

Scott's admiration for the chariot scenes staged by Yakima Canutt in *Ben-Hur*, arguably the most thrilling horse stunts ever, once again appears in the opening battle, full of chariot wrecks and gallantry, echoes *Ben-Hur* in Scott's selection of teams of white horses and black horses, which stand out brilliantly against the grimy backdrop of barbarian Germania. As usual, Scott's horses are more than simple vehicles, as they vocalize endlessly. A dying horse whimpers and huffs pathetically. Horses whinny and snort and react by rearing or running in dangerous situations. The scenes of the Egyptians traversing dangerous mountain roads in an attempt to catch up to the escaping Hebrews are fraught with danger, with horses and chariots tumbling off the roads en masse in realistic CGI.

The usual assortment of animals populates the frames of *Exodus*: cobras, crocodiles, camels, goats, sheep, dogs, and cats are everywhere, to create a realistic world, making one realize how underpopulated most historical films are and how animal life defines a historical period. Also as usual, the horses wear the finery of the era, and the infinite credits contain a horse tack modeler responsible for creating the horse armor and dressing. The horse master for the film, Daniel Naprous, who also worked on *Robin Hood*, was immediately co-opted to work on the television series *Game of Thrones* (2011– 2019), which entirely adopted the Ridley Scott attention to horses, stealing many shots outright. Horse trainer Tom Cox, who was also a stunt rider in *War Horse* and *Robin Hood*, followed Naprous to *Game of Thrones* to further utilize the Ridley Scott style of filming hordes of horses magnificently riding into battle. Without Ridley Scott, *Game of Thrones* might have been quite different and far less thrilling.

It is worth noting that Daniel Naprous is one of the owners of The Devil's Horsemen, the most prominent suppliers of horses to films made in Europe, along with his father, Gerard, and his sister, Camilla. They own more than one hundred horses trained to do specific stunts and perform as actors, and also own more than six hundred historic carriages and a vast collection of horse armor from various eras and of a variety of styles. The Devil's Horsemen provided the fourteen horses who played the heroic Joey in *War Horse*, and their ability to provide veteran acting horses and the accompanying tack makes them perfect for Ridley Scott's medieval and biblical universes.

The Devil's Horsemen again supplied horses, armor, and carts for Ridley Scott's 2021 medieval epic, *The Last Duel*, which debuted to ho-hum reviews and little box office success, resulting in a series of Scott interviews to publicize the film that were profanity-laced and condescending. Scott felt the merits of this film had been utterly misunderstood and blamed its lack of success on millennials who don't have the necessary patience for a rather slow-moving, historical and psychological tale. Scott was correct. The film—told, *Rashomon*-like, in alternating viewpoints that provide conflicting stories of the central element of the plot, the rape of Marguerite (Jodie Comer) by the dashing squire Le Gris (Adam Driver)—has both depth of character and the usual Scott utterly complete universe, as well as, of course, great horses. The movie is historically accurate, as the duel between Marguerite's husband, Carrouges (Matt Damon), and Le Gris was actually the last duel allowed in France. This of course echoes the obsession with honor of *The Duellists* (1977), but the filmmaker introduces a new element, that of the plight of women in 1386. They were bought and sold as wives, used by their husbands as property whose only value was the production of male heirs, and subjected to rape, which seems to have been a lifestyle for squires, knights, and nobility at court. Marguerite's desire to speak her truth and have justice done, though, is quite different from the male obsessiveness of *The Duellists*. She wants her truth to be known, and to have Le Gris punished appropriately, a squeak of feminism in this world where women have no power.

Previously Marguerite has been unable to conceive an heir for Carrouges, but after the rape, she is shown obviously pregnant. We also, during her point-of-view segment, know that Carrouges, rather than comforting her after she tells him of her rape by Le Gris, insists on immediate sexual intercourse, as if he could erase the rape by his husbandly attentions. Women are regarded as no more than broodmares, property owned by their husbands for reproductive purposes, and Scott makes this absolutely clear in one terrific scene that occurs during Marguerite's point-of-view segment and of course uses actual horses to create a perfect metaphor for the entire film.

In this scene, Carrouges takes Marguerite to see a new broodmare being held by a groom in a small paddock. He carelessly leaves the paddock gate open behind him (anyone who has handled horses knows to make sure all opened gates are closed or apocalypse may result) and begins to brag about his new gray mare's lineage of great war horses. He believes that her offspring will provide income for the farm. Marguerite, standing where Carrouges has placed her, a few feet in front of the mare, watches stonily.

Suddenly, a rampant, black stallion who has gotten loose from his handler careens into the paddock and instantly mounts the mare. Carrouges, furious, says that the mare is in heat and is meant to be bred to another stallion, so he picks up a shovel and begins hitting the stallion while the stallion has sex with the mare, eventually getting him to dismount the mare.

We hear nothing more of this incident until Marguerite, inspecting the horses in Carrouges's absence, pets the mare and says to her groom, "Her pregnancy is going well." But who is the father of the in utero foal? The wrong stallion, who staged a virtual rape of the mare (who was a huge fire-breathing black horse, important in Scott cosmology), or the right one? We have no idea. Just as when Marguerite, testifying before the court while obviously pregnant, doesn't know who fathered her child, Le Gris or Carrouges, though we suspect the wrong stallion in this case too, as in five years of married life and grim, grunting, rape-like sex with Carrouges, she has been unable to conceive. Marguerite is the mare, a piece of property, used for reproductive sex without any consideration for her own pleasure or desire, by both her husband and Le Gris. Her entire life is power-lessness and rape, and she is as much owned property as the gray mare. As a creature of her time and milieu, she was willing to accept this, even once captured in this marriage to an oaf only good at war (certainly not at sex), but when it became so painfully obvious that she was no more than property, just as the mare was, she rebelled and insisted that the truth of her abuse be known. This one small scene with the gray mare encapsulates the plight of women in this time and may spark a seed of awareness, of feminism in a nascent form, in Marguerite. Along with the great Ripley in *Alien* (1979) and like Thelma and Louise in their eponymous film (1991), Marguerite is one of Scott's terrific woman characters who want control of their own lives, and he illustrates this using his favorite symbol, the horse. Just as Scott has previously twinned his protagonists with noble horses, resulting in the characters being ennobled, here Marguerite's experience with a horse reveals to her the profundity of her power-lessness in this society, though she is ennobled in her quest for truth.

The titular duel features Scott's usual black and white horses, with Carrouges on a white and Le Gris on a black, but clearly there are no good guys here: only bad guys. The horses are adorned with gorgeous armor from the warehouses of The Devil's Horsemen and run at each other with courageous abandon, choreographed by Scott to perfection. At one point, as if it knows the importance of what's going on, Carrouges's horse rears and paws the air, desperate to get on with the action, though he will shortly find himself with a lance in his chest, murdered by Le Gris, and at this point the duel becomes man against man, neither with absolute right and goodness on his side. The best we can hope for is that Marguerite's life will be spared, even though that means rooting for the oafish Carrouges.

1492: Conquest of Paradise (1992)

Leave it to Ridley Scott to tell the story of Columbus's discovery of America, *1492: Conquest of Paradise* (1992), with two glorious horses secreted in the action. This horribly miscast film features French lout Gérard Depardieu as Columbus, complete with appalling English pronunciation, endless sweatiness, and an idée fixe that ends in many massacres. The title itself, *Conquest of Paradise*, must be ironic, because it is Paradise that makes a conquest of the Spaniards and other Europeans who attempt to civilize it. Depardieu is so lacking in any screen charisma that he is a black hole in the film, and it is simply disconcerting and unpleasant to have to look at him.

On the other hand, my favorite contemporary bad guy, Michael Wincott (1958–), he of the horse face and black mane and raspy voice and evil eye, plays Moxica, Columbus's archenemy, who fills the screen with his blackguard charisma and steals every scene he is in, but especially one scene with his typical black stallion (of course, as only heroes ride white horses in Scott-world). Horse master and stunt coordinator Greg Powell has the horse prancing, rearing, snorting, whinnying, and in general showing off with Wincott aboard, and the scene depicts the moment when the Indigenous people see a horse, and further, a man mounted on a horse, for the first time. Wincott and equine prompt a frenzy, reminiscent of teenage girls' first glimpses of the Beatles. The natives swarm the dancing, happy-footed animal and demon rider, jostling one another to get close to it, to lay hands on it. The scene suggests a spectacle beyond comprehension, the first glimpse of a centaur. Unfortunately, the entire film dies from an absence of charisma when Wincott dives off a cliff to his death, after fomenting a bloody, fiery mutiny against Columbus. He dies curiously garbed, in a black spangled outfit identifying him as the dude gunfighter of the film; while everyone else wears worn, sweat-stained work clothes, his clothes are as showy as his performance. All that we are left with is Depardieu, the last person you want to see on a big screen, with his inexplicable obsession with the New World as huge and fulsome as his acting is bad.

Earlier in the film, another stellar horse steals a scene. Armand Assante, as a counselor to Queen Isabella, is discussing Columbus with another member of the court, but because this is a Ridley Scott film, this discussion takes place with Assante aboard a stunning white horse that he is training in a round pen. He puts the horse through its paces, urging it to perform a gaited walk, spins, and rears, all while discussing politics. I can't remember a bit of this conversation, as my gaze fixated on the horse and its performance. Ridley Scott uses his usual palette of horse colors—he loves the contrast of black and white horses (no bays, browns, or chestnuts for him) and can't resist putting Wincott on the perfect bad guy's black horse. The film features the usual ark of Scott, with sheep, donkeys, dogs, oxen, camels, snakes, and exotic birds, but these two horses steal this flaccid show with ease.

Napoleon (2023)

Even Ridley Scott errs, however, and his film *Napoleon* doesn't seem to know what it wants to be: a war film, a biography, or a love story. Because of this, all three possible themes fail. And clearly Scott couldn't get enough of it: it is over three hours long, three hours of confusion. Even the horses aren't used well, with great numbers of them lined up, then running into battle, without a hint of understanding among them. In one scene, early on, with horses and riders lined up to charge into battle, all the horses remain still as statues, except for one. This one, a scene-stealer, tosses his head energetically, bored with the lack of action. There is a spectacularly exploding horse in battle in Toulon, which seems to harken back to the horses in the joust in *The Last Duel*, but that is clearly done with special effects rather than any understanding of the horse. Too much Joaquin Phoenix, and not enough horses: this is not the recipe for a great horse film.

The Duellists (1977)

I've saved Ridley Scott's debut film, *The Duellists* (1977), for last because in it is a scene that defines Scott's whole future work with horses, a scene that was undoubtedly unplanned and yet left in the film, underscoring Scott's love of horses and their sentience. A tale of the obsessive pursuit of honor to the point of ridiculousness, based on a Joseph Conrad short story, *The Duellists* demonstrates for the first time Scott's ability to re-create a period in history, in this case the Napoleonic Wars, and populates this world with geese, cows, cats, sheep, oxen, dogs, and even mice, and the horses in it vocalize frequently, whinnying and snorting in nearly every scene in which they appear. The horse master for the film, Richard Graydon, would find fame for his stunt doubling of James Bond in ten Bond films, demonstrating a fearlessness that even his fellow stuntmen admired, as well as working with director Nicholas Roeg in *The Man Who Fell to Earth* and *Don't Look Now*. He was known for his courage performing stunts at great heights, notably hanging on to a train car with one hand as that train wove through the Alps in *Moonraker*.

The Duellists was made on the cheap, for a budget rumored to be between $1.5 million and $1.9 million, with Scott himself having to pay for the completion bond; at this point, he had been a director of only television commercials, music videos, and a few episodes of television shows, and producers were reluctant to back him. The movie was shot quickly, in fifteen days, with Scott's own hotel room, dressed by himself and his art production staff, to stand in for multiple locations. As well, it was shot in winter, in Scotland—not a milieu conducive to filmmaking—and Scott frequently operated the single camera himself, getting whatever scenes he could in one take. Even at this very early stage in his career, the visual beauty and elegance of the film stand out, as does his re-creation of a historical era, despite budgetary constraints.

In the scene that epitomizes all of Scott's work to come with horses and is to my knowledge unique in all equine cinema, General

The Duellists, 1997. Christina Raines and Keith Carradine with a well-behaved gray horse. Directed by Ridley Scott. (Paramount Pictures/Photofest. ©Paramount Pictures.)

Hubert (Keith Carradine) and his sweetheart, the young neighbor Adele (Christina Raines), have ridden out to a sunlit meadow on matching pale gray horses. They dismount, and romance in the form of a marriage proposal is imminent. Hubert's horse, however, sniffs at the muzzle of Adele's horse and takes umbrage at something it perceives, pinning its ears and voicing a loud squeal. The horses continue to sniff at each other, ears pinned, and Carradine shushes his horse so he can get on with the scene, tugging at his horse's reins to get it to back up.

This odd "scream" uttered as a kind of warning to the other horse is instinctive dominance behavior. I've witnessed this behavior countless times, usually when a new mare challenges another mare's leadership or when I was teasing a cycling mare to determine her readiness for mating. The teasing horse would frequently squeal after sniffing at the mare, and sometimes the mare, not yet ready to go to the breeding shed, would squeal loudly in protest. This is instinctual behavior, and I don't believe that Richard Graydon taught these horses to interact in this way. It simply happened, and Carradine's attempt to shush the horses and keep them apart, while in character, demonstrates a certain amount of horse smarts. I imagine Scott, behind the single camera, trying to utilize the unusual bright sunlight to good effect, only to have naughty horses. So the constraints of money and weather surely made him want to use the take, as did Carradine's ability to remain in character though he seems aware that he might be in a real jackpot of kicking, rearing horses at any moment. But Scott, the horse lover, allows his enjoyment of the horses interacting to be as great as his enjoyment of the interaction of the humans about to commit to each other in marriage. I can think of no other film that has captured instinctive horse behavior and left it in the final cut, demonstrating Scott's good fortune and ability to put his knowledge of horses to work in this debut film, creating a moment in which horses vocalize and act, as they do in his other historical epics.

I can't help but imagine a Ridley Scott Warehouse of Horse Attire, where he has stored all of his historical horse garb for future use and because he has such tender feelings for the horses he uses in his films. How I would love to be given access to this warehouse! Scott dresses his horses as beautifully as he does his human stars, enhancing their gorgeousness and their sentience through horse clothes. If humans wear beautiful period garb, so must their horses in Scottlandia. Each horse is treated as an important character and clothed as such in period finery that enhances their acting. (Evidently, the Ridley Scott Warehouse of Horse Attire exists as a part of The Devil's Horsemen, though it isn't dedicated only to the great Scott, and it would be a magical place to visit.) Scott's belief in horse sentience shines in every one of his historical epics.

Epilogue
At the Wire

Attempting to see every horse movie that someone considered to be one of the best was a daunting task, but I felt I needed to get the strongest overview to organize these films into my Horse Hall of Fame. I chose using the concept of sentience, emotional and intellectual comprehension of what was going on around them, as my organizational tool because I quickly realized that my favorite horse films were those in which the horses were gifted anthropomorphically and that in the films I was watching, it does not take long to figure out which way the plot is gravitating. Who among us doesn't believe our pets have an almost human, if not superhuman, awareness of us and of their world? Having lived with and taken care of horses for decades, I knew this to be true of them, and needed to find the movies that expressed this. Of course, I got to the point that movies with horses acting simply as rider-mobiles upset me. What about the horse, I thought? What is the horse thinking? What is the horse trying to communicate?

Of course, horses also functioned as symbols, frequently of the main character, or as exemplars of status or theme, and clever writers and directors used them wisely as such. Horses represent a lot of movie screen time, so the use of them simply as transportation seemed foolish. Let them live as much as the human actors, with love and hate in their hearts and any other emotion you can imagine.

This book, then, became a glimpse for the uninitiated into the world of the true horse lover and a means of seeing this world as true horse lovers do as well as an indication of how horses see the world. Having lived with them for nearly three decades, I know they have opinions about nearly everything, just as we humans do. Horse consciousness is a real thing.

I have to reiterate here the main difference between our dogs and cats and our horses. Cats are pretty much solitary creatures. Dogs prefer to live in a pack, with a clearly defined leader. They are both predatory species and, because of this, are inherently without fear. Horses are different; they are a prey species and must be attuned to the outside world for ubiquitous danger. Because of this, they live in herds, and their protection of one another is a given. For a handler to single one out for the vet or farrier and take it away from its herd necessitates that the horse trusts this handler and bonds with her while the solitary work is being done. Horses must know they can trust us and communicate with us, or handling them singly would be impossible.

Thus the horse-human bond becomes all the more precious; the ability to allay a prey species animal's fear of being solitary is something truly beautiful. The best horse films portray this partnership of two emotionally intelligent species as significant and thrilling. The populating of a Horse Hall of Fame became easy with this as the criterion. Though, even without this bar, the loveliness of looking at beautiful horses is a reward in and of itself. Certain horses make you happy to be up and awake way too early; getting to regard them in their early morning paddocks and stalls becomes a reward in and of itself. They make one happy to be alive.

Acknowledgments

Patrick McGilligan must be first, as he is the true godfather of this book as well as my longtime friend and editor. My brother, film scholar Eric Smoodin, helped me in every way, at every step in the research and writing, and made suggestions of movies to see that I would never have thought of; his encyclopedic knowledge of film and his kindness know no bounds. Gwenda Young offered her insights into *National Velvet*, for which I am grateful. Similarly, Vincent LoBrutto offered insight into the work of Ridley Scott. Thanks, of course, to everyone at the University Press of Kentucky for their support, especially Ashley Runyon, the director, for taking a chance on my giddy enthusiasm for horses in the movies.

I canvassed friends, among them Debra Gorlin and Brad Crenshaw, Darlene Eliot, Jill Williams, and others I am undoubtedly forgetting, for their favorite horse movies, and they generously made suggestions. For their inspirational horse training, thanks to Bobby Lovgren, Rusty Hendrickson, and the Naprous family, whose amazing farm, The Devil's Horsemen, sits outside of London. Their evident belief in the possibility of sentient horses in movies fueled me in my development of the theme of this book.

Thanks too to the amazing archives of the American Morgan Horse Association, the *American Morgan Horse Magazine*, the National Museum of the Morgan Horse, and writer Brenda L. Tippin for revealing everything I needed to know about Rex as well as to the American Quarter Horse Association for articles on Docs Keepin Time.

Finally, kudos, gratitude, and love to Tim, who patiently watched countless movies with me and listened to all my enthusiastic discoveries, day by day, though he had no inherent interest in Yakima Canutt, Rex the Devil Horse, or *Into the West*. His support has meant everything to me.

And of course, thanks to all the horses whose lives I was privileged to share and care for, through good times and catastrophes. Thanks to Country Mama, Let's Punt (Sally), December Folie, Sweet Repent, Stormy Saratoga, Doctor Dora, and even to the evil Piroette, who taught me never to turn my back on her—good advice for all of life.

Filmography

1920: *The Mark of Zorro*, directed by Fred Niblo, produced by Douglas Fairbanks Production Company

1924: *The King of the Wild Horses*, directed by Fred Jackman, produced by Hal Roach

1925: *The Black Cyclone*, directed by Fred Jackman, produced by Hal Roach

1926: *The Devil Horse*, directed by Fred Jackman, produced by Hal Roach

1927: *No Man's Law*, directed by Fred Jackman, produced by Hal Roach

1933: *The Man from Monterey*, directed by Mack V. Wright, produced by Sid Rogell

1934: *The Star Packer*, directed by Robert N. Bradbury, produced by Monogram Pictures

1934: *Broadway Bill*, directed by Frank Capra, produced by Columbia Pictures

1934: *Little Miss Marker*, directed by Alexander Hall, produced by Paramount Pictures

1935: *The Adventures of Rex and Rinty*, directed by B. Reeves Eason and Ford Beebe, produced by Mascot Pictures

1936: *The Charge of the Light Brigade*, directed by Michael Curtiz, produced by Jack L. Warner and Hal B. Wallis

1937: *A Day at the Races*, directed by Sam Wood, produced by Warner Brothers

1938: *The Adventures of Robin Hood*, directed by Michael Curtiz and William Keighley, produced by Warner Brothers

1938: *Stablemates*, directed by Sam Wood, produced by Metro-Goldwyn-Mayer

1939: *Dodge City*, directed by Michael Curtiz, produced by Warner Brothers

1939: *Jesse James*, directed by Henry King, produced by 20th Century Studios

1939: *Stagecoach*, directed by John Ford, produced by Walter Wanger Productions

1940: *The Mark of Zorro*, directed by Rouben Mamoulian, produced by Darryl F. Zanuck

1940: *Virginia City*, directed by Michael Curtiz, produced by Warner Brothers

1943: *The Adventures of Baron Munchausen*, directed by Josef von Baky, produced by UFA

1943: *My Friend Flicka*, directed by Harold Schuster, produced by Twentieth Century Studios

1944: *National Velvet*, directed by Clarence Brown, produced by Metro-Goldwyn-Mayer

1946: *Beauty and the Beast*, directed by Jean Cocteau, produced by André Paulvé

1946: *Black Beauty*, directed by Max Nosseck, produced by 20th Century Fox

1946: *Notorious*, directed by Alfred Hitchcock, produced by David O. Selznick

1947: *Gallant Bess*, directed by Andrew Morton, produced by Metro-Goldwyn-Mayer

1948: *Fort Apache*, directed by John Ford, produced by Merian C. Cooper and John Ford

1948: *Red River*, directed and produced by Howard Hawks

1948: *The Adventures of Gallant Bess*, directed by Lew Landers, produced by Briskin and Rapf

1949: *She Wore a Yellow Ribbon*, directed by John Ford, produced by Merian C. Cooper

1950: *Riding High*, directed and produced by Frank Capra

1950: *Rio Grande*, directed by John Ford, produced by Merian C. Cooper and John Ford

1950: *Wagon Master*, directed by John Ford, produced by Merian C. Cooper and John Ford

1956: *Giant*, directed by George Stevens, produced by Henry Ginsberg and George Stevens

1956: *The Searchers*, directed by John Ford, produced by Merian C. Cooper and Patrick Ford

1961: *The Misfits*, directed by John Huston, produced by Frank E. Taylor and John Huston

1964: *Marnie*, directed and produced by Alfred Hitchcock

1965: *Cat Ballou*, directed by Elliot Silverstein, produced by Harold Hecht

1966: *El Dorado*, directed and produced by Howard Hawks

1969: *True Grit*, directed by Henry Hathaway, produced by Hal B. Wallis

1969: *The Wild Bunch*, directed by Sam Peckinpah, produced by Warner Brothers

1973: *Pat Garret and Billy the Kid*, directed by Sam Peckinpah, produced by Gordon Carroll

1975: *Bite the Bullet*, directed by Richard Brooks, produced by Columbia Pictures

1976: *The Shootist*, directed by Don Siegel, produced by M. J. Frankovich

1977: *The Duellists*, directed by Ridley Scott, produced by David Puttnam

1979: *The Black Stallion*, directed by Carroll Ballard, produced by Francis Ford Coppola

1980: *The Long Riders*, directed by Walter Hill, produced by James Keach and Stacy Keach

1983: *Phar Lap*, directed by Simon Wincer, produced by Hoyts Edgley Company

1985: *Silverado*, directed and produced by Lawrence Kasdan

1988: *The Adventures of Baron Munchausen*, directed by Terry Gilliam, produced by Allied Filmmakers

1990: *Dances with Wolves*, directed by Kevin Costner, produced by Kevin Costner and Jim Wilson

1991: *Robin Hood: Prince of Thieves*, directed by Kevin Reynolds, produced by Morgan Creek Entertainment and Warner Brothers

1992: *1492: Conquest of Paradise*, directed and produced by Ridley Scott

1992: *Into the West*, directed by Mike Newell, produced by Miramax

1992: *Unforgiven*, directed and produced by Clint Eastwood

1993: *Tombstone*, directed by George P. Cosmatos, produced by Hollywood Pictures and Cinergi Pictures

1994: *Black Beauty*, directed by Caroline Thompson, produced by Constantin Film

1994: *Wyatt Earp*, directed by Lawrence Kasdan, produced by Kasdan Brothers, Tig Productions, and Warner Brothers

1998: *The Horse Whisperer*, directed by Robert Redford, produced by Touchstone Pictures

1998: *The Mask of Zorro*, directed by Martin Campbell, produced by Tri Star Pictures and Amblin Entertainment

1999: *Shergar*, directed by Martin Campbell, produced by Blue Rider Pictures

1999: *Simpatico*, directed by Matthew Warchus, produced by Studiocanal

2000: *All the Pretty Horses*, directed by Billy Bob Thornton, produced by Miramax

2000: *Gladiator*, directed by Ridley Scott, produced by DreamWorks Pictures, Scott Free Productions, and Universal Pictures

2001: *The Lord of the Rings: The Fellowship of the Ring*, directed by Peter Jackson, produced by Peter Jackson and Warner Brothers

2002: *The Lord of the Rings: The Two Towers*, directed by Peter Jackson, produced by Peter Jackson and Warner Brothers

2003: *The Lord of the Rings: The Return of the King*, directed by Peter Jackson, produced by Peter Jackson and Warner Brothers

2003: *Seabiscuit*, directed by Gary Ross, produced by Universal Pictures and DreamWorks Pictures

2004: *Hidalgo*, directed by Joe Johnston, produced by Touchstone Pictures

2005: *Dreamer*, directed by John Gatins, produced by Michael Tollin and Brian Robbins

2005: *Kingdom of Heaven*, directed and produced by Ridley Scott

2005: *The Legend of Zorro*, directed by Martin Campbell, produced by Columbia Pictures and Amblin Entertainment

2007: *The Assassination of Jesse James by the Coward Robert Ford*, directed by Andrew Dominik, produced by Plan B Entertainment and Warner Brothers

2007: *No Country for Old Men*, directed by the Coen Brothers, produced by Paramount Vantage and Miramax

2008: *Appaloosa*, directed by Ed Harris, produced by New Line Cinema

2010: *Robin Hood*, directed by Ridley Scott, produced by Imagine Entertainment, Relativity Media, and Scott Free Productions

2010: *Secretariat*, directed by Randall Wallace, produced by Fast Track Productions, Mayhem Pictures, and Walt Disney Productions

2010: *True Grit*, directed by the Coen Brothers, produced by Mike Zoss Productions, Skydance Media, Paramount Pictures, DreamWorks Pictures, Amblin Entertainment, and Scott Rudin Productions

2011: *Buck*, directed by Cindy Meehle, produced by Cedar Creek Productions, Back Allie Productions, and Motto Pictures

2011: *War Horse*, directed by Steven Spielberg, produced by Touchstone Pictures, Emblin Entertainment, and DreamWorks Pictures

2013: *The Lone Ranger*, directed by Gore Verbinsky, produced by Jerry Bruckheimer Films, Bliind Wink Films, Walt Disney Pictures, and Infinitum Nihil

2014: *Exodus: Gods and Kings*, directed by Ridley Scott, produced by Scott Free Productions, Babieka, and Chemin Entertainment

2014: *50 to 1*, directed and produced by Jim Wilson

2014: *Winter's Tale*, directed and produced by Akiva Goldsman

2015: *Dark Horse*, directed by Louise Osmond, produced by Sony Picture Classics

2015: *Slow West*, directed by John Maclean, produced by See-Saw Films, DMC Films, Film 4 Productions, New Zealand Film Commission, and Rachel Gardner Films

2020: *Dream Horse*, directed by Euros Lyn, produced by Cornerstone Films, Film4, Raw, and Ingenious

2021: *Concrete Cowboy*, directed by Ricky Staub, produced by Tucker Tooley Entertainment

2021: *The Last Duel*, directed by Ridley Scott, produced by Scott Free Productions and Twentieth Century Fox Studios

2021: *The Power of the Dog*, directed by Gillian Armstrong, produced by See-Saw Films, New Zealand Film Commission, Cross City Films, and BBC Films

2023: *Napoleon*, directed by Ridley Scott, produced by Apple Studios and Scott Free Productions

Notes

1. Muybridge and the Wonder Ponies

Details about Eadweard Muybridge and his inventions are drawn from Hans Christian Adam's *Eadweard Muybridge: The Human and Animal Locomotion Photographs* (Cologne: Taschen, 2010).

The foundational information about the start of film is drawn from Thomas Hagener Elsaesser's "The Birth of Cinema: Lumiere Brothers and George Melies," *Screen and Sound Magazine*, March 3, 2016.

Marey's different approach to infant film is drawn from Francois Dagognet's *E. J. Marey: A Passion for the Trace* (Brooklyn, NY: Zone Books, 1992).

References to westerns are drawn from John Howard Reid's *Great Hollywood Westerns: Classic Pictures, Must-See Movies & "B" Films* (Everand E Books online, 2011).

2. Rex, the Devil Horse

The firsthand accounts of Rex the Devil Horse attempting murder are drawn from Yakima Canutt's *My Rodeo Years: Memoir of a Bronc Rider's Path to Hollywood Fame* (Jefferson, NC: McFarland, 2010) and *Stunt Man: The Autobiography of Yakima Canutt* (Norman: University of Oklahoma Press, 1979).

Harry Carey Jr.'s account of Rex attempting murder and general outlaw behavior on film sets is drawn from Harry Carey Jr.'s *Company of Heroes: My Life as an Actor in the John Ford Stock Company* (Lanham, MD: Scarecrow Press, 1994).

Biographical information on Charles "Chick" Morrison and Jack "Swede" Lindell is drawn from IMDb (International Movie Database), online. These two men discovered and trained the evil Rex.

The history and movie career of Rex and information on the Morgan Horse is from the American Morgan Horse Association archives in Lexington, Kentucky.

3. John Wayne, the Godfather of All Movie Horses

Information on John Wayne's stuntman is drawn from Yakima Canutt's *Stunt Man: The Autobiography of Yakima Canutt* (Norman: University of Oklahoma Press, 1979).

Information on John Wayne is drawn from Scott Eyman's *John Wayne: The Life and Legend* (New York: Simon and Schuster, 2014), the definitive history of the actor who defined and represented the entire genre of westerns.

Harry Carey Jr.'s experience of working on a film with John Wayne is drawn from Harry Carey Jr.'s *Company of Heroes: My Life as an Actor in the John Ford Stock Company* (Lanham, MD: Scarecrow Press, 1994).

Biographical information on actor and stuntman Ben Johnson, the greatest rider in westerns, ever, is drawn from IMDb online.

Biographical information on the great director John Ford is drawn from IMDb online.

The account of how Ben Johnson discovered Hollywood is drawn from Marshall Trimble's "Ben Johnson: A True American Cowboy," *True West Magazine*, September 2021.

4. A Day at the Races

The historical account of all the movie people who attended and loved horse racing is drawn from Alan Shuback's *Hollywood at the Races: Film's Love Affair with the Turf* (Lexington: University Press of Kentucky, 2019).

The descriptions of Capra's films, including the two made about horse racing, are drawn from Eric Smoodin's *Regarding Frank Capra: Audience, Celebrity, and American Film Studies, 1930–1960* (Durham, NC: Duke University Press, 2004).

Information and insight into the iconic comedian and his day spent at the races is drawn from Groucho Marx's *Groucho and Me* (Los Angeles, CA: Gels Associates, 1959).

Biographical information on stars from the film *Stablemates*, Wallace Beery and Mickey Rooney, is drawn from IMDb online.

The real story behind Big Red is drawn from William Nack's *Secretariat* (New York: Hyperion, 1975), the classic, best history of the champion racehorse.

Information on Seabiscuit is drawn from Lauren Hillenbrand's *Seabiscuit: An American Legend* (New York: Ballantine Books, 2002), the complete history of the great racehorse.

Information on the unique group of stunt people and the horses they've trained is drawn from The Devil's Horsemen online (https://thedevilshorsemen.com/).

Information on Harpo Marx's riding ability is drawn from Harpo Marx's *Harpo Speaks* (Hamburg: Albatross, 2019).

Information on the historical Canadian races that the great horses ran in is drawn from an untitled article in *Canadian Thoroughbred Magazine* by Andrew Hanna from June 2021.

5. Girls and Their Horses

Essential information about the making of *National Velvet* from the film's director is drawn from Gwenda Young's *Clarence Brown: Hollywood's Forgotten Master* (Lexington: University Press of Kentucky, 2018).

Information about the involvement of Ralph McCutcheon, Highland Dale, Elizabeth Taylor, Shirley Temple, Kelly Reno, and Martin Scorsese in the film *Giant* is all drawn from IMDb online.

The history behind the life and movie roles of actress Elizabeth Taylor is drawn from Kate Andersen Brower's *Elizabeth Taylor: The Grit and Glamour of an Icon* (New York: Harper, 2022).

The story of a real-life horse whisperer, on whom the character in the book and movie may have been based, is drawn from Monty Roberts's *The Man Who Listens to Horses* (New York: Ballantine Books, 2008).

Information on the making of *Little Miss Marker* is drawn from Shirley Temple Black's *Child Star: An Autobiography* (New York: McGraw Hill, 1988).

Information on the making of *Marnie* is drawn from Patrick McGilligan's *Alfred Hitchcock: A Life in Darkness and Light* (New York: It Books, a division of Harper Collins, 2004).

6. Magical Horses

Biographical information on Caleb Deschanel, Bobby Lovgren, Mike Newell, and Terry Gilliam is drawn from IMDb online.

7. Heartstrings

Discussion on Clark Gable's death is drawn from David Niven's *Bring On the Empty Horses* (London: Hodder and Stouten, 1975).

Information on the Coen brothers' remaking of the classic *True Grit* is drawn from IMDb online.

Biographical and other film-related information on Friedrich von Lebeder, *War Horse*, Highland Dale, and Rex Petersen is drawn from IMDb online.

Information on directing the great stars in *The Misfits* is drawn from John Huston's *An Open Book* (New York: Knopf, 1980), an autobiography that must certainly have some tall tales in it but that is also very informative and interesting.

Information on Anna Sewell and *Black Beauty* is drawn from Adrienne Gavin's *Dark Horse: A Life of Anna Sewell* (Stroud, UK: Sutton, 2004).

8. Kevin Costner and Other Hunks on Horses

Biographical information on Kevin Costner, Lawrene Kasdan, Rex Petersen, and Viggo Mortensen is drawn from IMDb online.

Information on Hidalgo and his rapscallion rider is drawn from Janice Ledendorf's *Searching for the Real Frank T. Hopkins* (New York: Create Space Independent Publishers, 2018), an attempt to sort out the lies and truths in the life of this man who inspired *Hidalgo*.

Background on the famous California Robin Hood is drawn from Husan Hsu's "The Legend of Joaquin Murrietta," *The Paris Review*, July 2018.

9. Horse Whisperers

Biographical information on Rex Peterson, Robert Redford, Buck Brannaman, and Billy Bob Thornton is drawn from IMDb online.

Plot information on *All the Pretty Horses* is drawn from Cormac McCarthy's *All The Pretty Horses* (New York: Knopf, 1992), the National Book Award–winning book on which the Academy Award–winning movie is based.

10. Ridley Scott and Horses

Ridley Scott in his own words is drawn from Lawrence F. Knapp and Andrea F. Kulas's *Ridley Scott: Interviews* (Jackson: University Press of Mississippi, 2005).

Biographical data on Ridley Scott and analysis of his films is drawn from Vincent LoBrutto's *Ridley Scott: A Biography* (Lexington: University Press of Kentucky, 2019).

The filmography of Ridley Scott is drawn from Ian Nathan's *Ridley Scott: A Retrospective* (London: Palazzo, 2020).

Bibliography

Auerbach, Ann Hagedorn. *Wild Ride: The Rise and Tragic Fall of Calumet Farm Inc., America's Premier Racing Dynasty.* New York: Henry Holt, 1995.

Canutt, Yakima. *My Rodeo Years: Memoir of a Bronc Rider's Path to Hollywood Fame.* Jefferson, NC: McFarland, 2009.

Canutt, Yakima, and Oliver Drake. *Stunt Man: The Autobiography of Yakima Canutt with Oliver Drake.* Norman: University of Oklahoma Press, 1997.

Carey, Harry, Jr. *Company of Heroes: My Life as an Actor in the John Ford Stock Company.* Lanham, MD: Scarecrow Press, 1996.

Eyman, Scott. *John Wayne: The Life and Legend.* New York: Simon and Schuster, 2015.

Flynn, Errol. *My Wicked, Wicked Ways: The Autobiography of Errol Flynn.* New York: Cooper Square Press, 2002.

Freeman, David. *Last Days of Alfred Hitchcock: A Memoir Featuring the Screenplay of "Alfred Hitchcock's The Short Night."* New York: Overlook Books, 1984.

Hillenbrand, Laura. *Seabiscuit: An American Legend.* New York: Ballantine Books, 2002.

Knapp, Laurence F., and Andrea F. Kulas. *Ridley Scott Interviews.* Jackson: University Press of Mississippi, 2005.

LoBrutto, Vincent. *Ridley Scott: A Biography.* Lexington: University Press of Kentucky, 2019.

Meyers, Jeffrey. *Inherited Risk: Errol and Sean Flynn in Hollywood and Vietnam*. New York: Simon and Schuster, 2002.

Mitchum, Patrine Day. *Hollywood Hoofbeats: A Celebration of Horses in Classic Movies and TV*. Irvine, CA: i5 Publishing, 2005.

Nack, William. *Secretariat: The Making of a Champion*. New York: Hyperion, 1988.

Nathan, Ian. *Ridley Scott: A Retrospective*. London: Palazzo, 2020.

Niven, David. *Bring on the Empty Horses*. New York: Dell, 1976.

Portis, Charles. *True Grit: A Novel*. New York: Simon and Schuster, 1968.

Pramaggiore, Maria. *Irish and African American Cinema: Identifying Others and Performing Identities, 1980–2000*. Albany: State University of New York Press, 2007.

Savage, Thomas. *The Power of the Dog*. Boston: Little, Brown, 1967.

Sewell, Anna. *Black Beauty*. London: Jarrold and Sons, 1877.

Smoodin, Eric. *Regarding Frank Capra: Audience, Celebrity, and American Film Studies, 1930–1960*. Durham, NC: Duke University Press, 2004.

Truffaut, Francois. *Hitchcock/Truffaut*. New York: Simon and Schuster, 1985.

Tyler, Parker. *Sex, Psyche, Etcetera in the Film*. London: Penguin, 1969.

Young, Gwenda. *Clarence Brow: Hollywood's Forgotten Master*. Lexington: University Press of Kentucky, 2018.

Index

Screen Classics

Screen Classics is a series of critical biographies, film histories, and analytical studies focusing on neglected filmmakers and important screen artists and subjects, from the era of silent cinema through the golden age of Hollywood to the international generation of today. Books in the Screen Classics series are intended for scholars and general readers alike. The contributing authors are established figures in their respective fields. This series also serves the purpose of advancing scholarship on film personalities and themes with ties to Kentucky.

Series Editor   Patrick McGilligan

Books in the Series

Olivia de Havilland: Lady Triumphant
    Victoria Amador
Mae Murray: The Girl with the Bee-Stung Lips
    Michael G. Ankerich
Harry Dean Stanton: Hollywood's Zen Rebel
    Joseph B. Atkins
Hedy Lamarr: The Most Beautiful Woman in Film
    Ruth Barton
Rex Ingram: Visionary Director of the Silent Screen
    Ruth Barton
Conversations with Classic Film Stars: Interviews from Hollywood's Golden Era
    James Bawden and Ron Miller
Conversations with Legendary Television Stars: Interviews from the First Fifty Years
    James Bawden and Ron Miller
They Made the Movies: Conversations with Great Filmmakers
    James Bawden and Ron Miller
You Ain't Heard Nothin' Yet: Interviews with Stars from Hollywood's Golden Era
    James Bawden and Ron Miller
Charles Boyer: The French Lover
    John Baxter
Von Sternberg
    John Baxter
Hitchcock's Partner in Suspense: The Life of Screenwriter Charles Bennett
    Charles Bennett, edited by John Charles Bennett
Hitchcock and the Censors
    John Billheimer
The Magic Hours: The Films and Hidden Life of Terrence Malick
    John Bleasdale
A Uniquely American Epic: Intimacy and Action, Tenderness and Violence in Sam Peckinpah's The Wild Bunch
    Edited by Michael Bliss

My Life in Focus: A Photographer's Journey with Elizabeth Taylor and the Hollywood Jet Set
Gianni Bozzacchi with Joey Tayler
Hollywood Divided: The 1950 Screen Directors Guild Meeting and the Impact of the Blacklist
Kevin Brianton
He's Got Rhythm: The Life and Career of Gene Kelly
Cynthia Brideson and Sara Brideson
Ziegfeld and His Follies: A Biography of Broadway's Greatest Producer
Cynthia Brideson and Sara Brideson
Eleanor Powell: Born to Dance
Paula Broussard and Lisa Royère
The Marxist and the Movies: A Biography of Paul Jarrico
Larry Ceplair
Dalton Trumbo: Blacklisted Hollywood Radical
Larry Ceplair and Christopher Trumbo
Warren Oates: A Wild Life
Susan Compo
Helen Morgan: The Original Torch Singer and Ziegfeld's Last Star
Christopher S. Connelly
Improvising Out Loud: My Life Teaching Hollywood How to Act
Jeff Corey with Emily Corey
Crane: Sex, Celebrity, and My Father's Unsolved Murder
Robert Crane and Christopher Fryer
Jack Nicholson: The Early Years
Robert Crane and Christopher Fryer
Anne Bancroft: A Life
Douglass K. Daniel
Being Hal Ashby: Life of a Hollywood Rebel
Nick Dawson
Bruce Dern: A Memoir
Bruce Dern with Christopher Fryer and Robert Crane
Intrepid Laughter: Preston Sturges and the Movies
Andrew Dickos
The Woman Who Dared: The Life and Times of Pearl White, Queen of the Serials
William M. Drew
Miriam Hopkins: Life and Films of a Hollywood Rebel
Allan R. Ellenberger
Vitagraph: America's First Great Motion Picture Studio
Andrew A. Erish
Jayne Mansfield: The Girl Couldn't Help It
Eve Golden
John Gilbert: The Last of the Silent Film Stars
Eve Golden
Strictly Dynamite: The Sensational Life of Lupe Velez
Eve Golden
Stuntwomen: The Untold Hollywood Story
Mollie Gregory
Jean Gabin: The Actor Who Was France
Joseph Harriss

Some Like It Wilder: The Life and Controversial Films of Billy Wilder
Gene D. Phillips
Ann Dvorak: Hollywood's Forgotten Rebel
Christina Rice
Mean . . . Moody . . . Magnificent! Jane Russell and the Marketing of a Hollywood Legend
Christina Rice
Fay Wray and Robert Riskin: A Hollywood Memoir
Victoria Riskin
Lewis Milestone: Life and Films
Harlow Robinson
Michael Curtiz: A Life in Film
Alan K. Rode
Ryan's Daughter: The Making of an Irish Epic
Paul Benedict Rowan
Arthur Penn: American Director
Nat Segaloff
Film's First Family: The Untold Story of the Costellos
Terry Chester Shulman
Claude Rains: An Actor's Voice
David J. Skal with Jessica Rains
June Mathis: The Rise and Fall of a Silent Film Visionary
Thomas J. Slater
Horses of Hollywood
Roberta Smoodin
Barbara La Marr: The Girl Who Was Too Beautiful for Hollywood
Sherri Snyder
Lionel Barrymore: Character and Endurance in Hollywood's Golden Age
Kathleen Spaltro
Buzz: The Life and Art of Busby Berkeley
Jeffrey Spivak
Victor Fleming: An American Movie Master
Michael Sragow
Aline MacMahon: Hollywood, the Blacklist, and the Birth of Method Acting
John Stangeland
My Place in the Sun: Life in the Golden Age of Hollywood and Washington
George Stevens Jr.
Hollywood Presents Jules Verne: The Father of Science Fiction on Screen
Brian Taves
Thomas Ince: Hollywood's Independent Pioneer
Brian Taves
Picturing Peter Bogdanovich: My Conversations with the New Hollywood Director
Peter Tonguette
Jessica Lange: An Adventurer's Heart
Anthony Uzarowski
Carl Theodor Dreyer and Ordet: My Summer with the Danish Filmmaker
Jan Wahl